AT 47

(Poems on Anything from Pussy Cats to Politics and Post Modernism)

By

Richard John Smith

http://www.rjs-tutor.co.uk/

Produced by Richard John Smith
Director of *R1 Publications* and the *Problem Solving Teaching Services* web site at http://www.rjs-tutor.co.uk/

Author of *The Exit Machine*

Storefront

http://www.lulu.com/spotlight/R1Publications

Soft cover editions may also be available through Amazon and other International Book Distributors by the end of February 2012.

ACKNOWLEDGEMENTS

Particular thanks are reserved for the various students and other contacts within the teaching profession who provided criticism and other forms of help.

Thanks are also given to local contacts that from October 2007 to November 2011 provided me with a multiplicity of venues to recite some of the poems in this collection. Their encouragement has been much appreciated.

AT 47

Produced by Richard John Smith
Director of *R1 Publications* and the *Problem Solving Teaching Services*
web site at http://www.rjs-tutor.co.uk/

Copyright © the Author 2008

All Rights Reserved,
The Moral Right of the author has been asserted and
covers all material produced before 2008.

First Released for Distribution by Lulu Publishing
December 2008

Second Trial Edition July 2011

Third International Edition November 2011

ISBN: 978-1-907910-06-7

CONTENTS

Preface XIII

PART A: BY POPULAR REQUEST 1

Prologue: By Popular Request 3

1. At Forty-Seven 4
2. Bitter The Night 5
3. Black Snake Motorway 6
4. Blade 8
5. Blood Red Battle 9
6. Boy! 9
7. British Creed 10
8. Bullet 12
9. Butterfly Blair 13
10. Café Pianco 14
11. Careerist Poet 15
12. Christmas Pleasures 16
13. Click 18
14. Climate Change 22
15. Damn The Critics 23
16. Denial 25

17. Drink 26

18. Entanglements 27

19. Exam Fatigue 28

20. Fame Train 29

21. Family politics 30

22. Flash, Crash, Dash 31

23. From Here I Begin 35

24. Genocide 35

25. Gentle Fire 35

26. Girl With The Broken Soul 36

27. Glacier 37

28. Glad To See You Go 38

29. Goal! 39

30. Goodbye Mr Guff 40

31. Gone 41

32. Green And Pleasant Land 42

33. Hay Fever Misery 43

34. Highland Vista 46

35. House, Mouse, Rouse 48

36. Hurry! Hurry! Hurry! 51

37.	I Protest	53
38.	If my Cat could Speak	54
39.	If You Say	56
40.	Ilkley Haiku 1	58
41.	Ilkley Haiku 2	59
42.	ISBN Nightmare	60
43.	Land Of Paradox	61
44.	Last Holiday With My Youngest Son	64
45.	Leeds Louts	65
46.	Love Fever	65
47.	Lovely Lizard	66
48.	Lovely Wife	68
49.	Mad Woman	69
50.	Match Stick Loneliness	70
51.	Matching Colours	71
52.	Meltdown	72
53.	Metro Class-Scape	74
54.	Misdirected Compliments	75
55.	Missing Missy	76
56.	Missy! Missy!	78

VIII

57. Morning Mail — 81
58. Multiple Surrender — 82
59. News Impact — 83
60. Night Wind — 85
61. Nightfall At Scarborough — 89
62. Nightmare Shopping — 91
63. No, My Dear — 92
64. Northern Scotland — 93
65. Oh, Mr Blair — 96
66. Old Brown Book — 97
67. Order of Conversation — 98
68. Perplexity — 99
69. Post Modern Blues — 100
70. Proof Reading Wife — 103
71. Reinstatement — 105
72. Reprise: At Forty-Seven — 106
73. Resisting the Waters — 106
74. Ruined Minds — 107
75. Seven Ages of Man — 108
76. Seven Women — 108

77. Shoreline Debris 109

78. Spin Doctor 110

79. Target 112

80. Teenage Tory Dreams 113

81. The Absent Muse 115

82. The Ancestral Mill 119

83. The Empty Bedroom 121

84. The Gathering 122

85. The Jolly Hobgoblin 124

86. The Local Fox 126

87. The Normal Poet 128

88. The Old, Old, Cat 130

89. The Unwanted Caller 131

90. Things 131

91. Thirteen Signs 132

92. Three Wishes 134

93. To My Father 135

94. Too Busy 136

95. Trashed 137

96. Tweedlecam and Tweedleclegg 138

97. Two Lovely Cats 139

98. Typhoon Tidal Wave 142

99. Unwanted Compliments 143

100. Was It? 145

101. Wedlock Hemlock 146

102. What Do I See? 147

103. What Do Women Want? 148

104. What Use? 150

105. When He Was Born 153

106. Who are those Men? 154

107. Wife Life! 155

108. Wife! Wife! 156

109. Winter Traffic 158

110. Wit 158

111. You Are 159

Epilogue: New Things 159

PART B: FOUR SEASONS 161

Prelude: Something for All Seasons 163

1. Dying Autumn 164

2. Gridlock Winter 165

3. Resurrection Spring ... 168

4. Spurn-Head Summer ... 170

5. Postlude: Seasonal Relaxation ... 173

PART C: LOOPY LIMERICKS ... 175

1. Cat Limericks ... 177

2. Limericks on Walking & Walkers ... 178

3. Party Conference Limericks ... 179

4. Forgotten Birthday ... 180

PART D: THE SILVER POEMS ... 181

1. Returning Memories ... 183

2. Strange Mystery ... 184

3. Twenty-Five ... 185

PART E: WITH LOVE TO PENELOPE ... 189

1. Lament for Penelope ... 191

2. Still Beauty ... 192

3. Farewell ... 193

4. Comfort ... 194

5. Turmoil-On-The-Boil ... 195

6. Where? ... 198

7. As ... 199

8. Gusting Heavenwards — 200

9. Hope — 201

10. Train carriage Doze — 202

PART F: SHORT STORIES — 203

1. A Patch of Green — 205

2. Bad Man — 209

3. Loner — 213

4. Recriminations — 218

5. The Muchworth Room — 228

6. Whitby Storm — 239

PART G: TEACHING AIDS — 245

1. How to Interpret Poetry — 247

2. How to Assess a Poem — 249

3. Advice to a Young Poet — 251

FURTHER READING — 257

1. Book List — 257

2. Booklets — 259

PREFACE

Following repeated requests from professional and personal contacts, I decided reproduce samples of my poetry in book form and here is the result. It's hoped that *'At 47'* will amuse, challenge, inform and motivate the reader. In addition, it aims to: -

1) Appeal to many people by presenting intriguing and well-constructed poetry

2) Be easily adapted to other forms of media

3) Celebrate the genuinely good things in life

4) Explore a diverse range of emotions and topics (some of them controversial)

5) Provide useful material for English Students or those starting out in poetry

6) Make some contribution to English Literature

7) Offer useful information on a variety of topics

8) Provide a chance for people to engage with the English Language

9) Satirise human pretence and hypocrisy

10) Stimulate thought by offering fresh and unusual perspectives.

Most of the poems in this collection were produced from May 2003 until December 2010. This was at a time when I was pleasantly surprised at discovering that a demand existed for my literary work (as reflected in the *'Prologue'* and my first poem, entitled *'At Forty Seven'*). Since October 2007, many opportunities have arisen to give public recitals of my poetry at different venues within my locality (one of which is celebrated in *'Cafe Pianco'*). I have also given recitals at two Literary Festivals held in Yorkshire.

A key characteristic of this collection is the variability in both style and subject matter. In **Part A** especially, readers just do not know what is coming next. A happy go-lucky poem about a pussycat could easily be followed by something abstract on Post Modernism; a sad poem involving death could be followed by a biting satire on some aspect of Britain's contemporary political and social scene. A conscious attempt has been made to explore a wide range of emotions and topics. Reflected are the unpredictable *'ups and downs'* of life.

Readers should note that in some poems an attempt has been made to adopt a *'persona,'* one expressing views which the reader may find unacceptable. These views do not necessarily reflect those of the author and he will not enter into debate over them.

For ease of reference most major collections have been placed in alphabetical order. The only exception was **Part E** where the material was arranged in chronological in order to highlight the sequence of events which occurred around a crucial domestic event.

Enclosed in **Part G** are the summary guides *'How to Interpret Poetry'* and a *'Poetry Criticism Questionnaire.'* English Students and novice poets should find these resources helpful. In contrast, *'The Advice to a Young Poet'* is couched in the form of ancient wisdom sayings in order to encourage thought and careful reflection.

Details of my private tutoring services can be found at http://www.rjs-tutor.co.uk/ (Please note they are confined to the Leeds-Bradford and Harrogate-Wakefield areas of West Yorkshire in the United Kingdom.)

Richard Smith
(Friday, 4th November 2011)

PART A: BY POPULAR REQUEST

(Miscellaneous Poems Covering a Wide Range of Human
Emotions and Situations)

2

PROLOGUE BY POPULAR REQUEST

By popular request I bring you my poems
By popular request I bring you my stories
By popular request I bring you my thoughts

So relax, enjoy yourselves,
Forget your worries and be prepared to be entertained
Or at least informed (hopefully)![1]

---

[1] This piece was written on Thursday, May 29th 2003, whilst travelling on a National Coach to Manchester. Its theme is the need to relax by reading light literature.

AT FORTY-SEVEN

At forty-seven
I discovered
I was a Poet.
Didn't want it!
Didn't expect it!

But at forty-seven
I was too old for romance
Too old for youthful ideals

At forty-seven
I discovered
Aching joints in my wrist
A dull throbbing in my back

At forty-seven
I discovered
Shortness of breath –
Must catch that nap!

Yet –
At forty-seven
I discovered
I was a poet
Where words exploded from my heart
Wonderland vistas opening up

And –
At forty-seven

I'm ready to begin.[2]

---

[2] This piece was written in my bedroom on the morning of Wednesday, May 28th 2003 and heavily revised following the suggestions of another poet on Friday, May 13th 2005. Its theme is the joy of discovering new talents in middle age.

BITTER THE NIGHT

Bitter was the night our love died,
Bitter was the night you packed your case
Bitter was the night you yelled *'goodbye!'*
Bitter was the night you slammed the door,

Bitter is the night in my soul[3]

---

[3] This piece was written on Saturday, 25th September 2005 after a walk around Kirkstall Abbey. Its theme is the bitter emotional effect of a broken relationship.

BLACK SNAKE MOTORWAY

The black rain pours down
Sheeting, sheeting
From a pitch black sky

The black rain pours down
Weeping, weeping
For the havoc it will cause

The black rain pours down
Turning, turning
Into white flecks of blinding snow

The black rain pours down
Sleeting, sleeting
Exploding into a myriad million water bombs

The black rain pours down
Running, running
Over the ice patches forming on the death trap motorway

The black rain pours down
Performing, performing
A death rattle on many a windscreen

The black rain pours down
Deluging, deluging
An already water logged moorland

The black rain pours down
Slowing, slowing
To a crawl, regimented lines of vehicles

The black rain pours down
Frustrating, frustrating
Many a busy schedule

The black rain pours down
Cleansing, Cleansing
The back of the Black Snake Motorway

The black rain pours down
The sky sheds tears
For tonight's roadside fatalities[4]

---

[4] This piece was written on the snowy evening of Saturday, 7th February 2004, just before the writer saw the crash scene mentioned in 'The Gathering.' It was shortened and revised in response to criticism on Friday, December 17th 2004 (with the last verse being added on Thursday, 5th February 2009). Its theme is the way bad weather on a motorway can frustrate human plans by seriously delaying road traffic.

BLADE

My name is *'Blade'*
I exist almost anywhere
I grow very slowly or
I can grow very fast

Trodden underfoot I maybe
Covered by every form of waste
I sometimes am
But soon
I spring back to life

My growth is inevitable
My expansion invincible
Vast territories I invade and rule
Why, I can even overturn the works of man

Nothing can stop me
Nothing can resist me
Nothing can halt me
For
I rapidly adapt to changing conditions

One day the whole world
Will be covered by my green mantle
Because
I am one of many

You may tread me underfoot for now
But in the end
I will always conquer
Because
I am part of the mighty species
Called *'grass'*[5]

---

[5] This poem was written on Thursday, 23rd April 2009

BLOOD RED BATTLE

Belt buckled tight
Breastplate clamped on
Shoes stoutly tied
Shield tilted up
Razor sharp sword
Ready in hand

Doors heaved open
Light shining through
Crowd's bloodlust roar

Fight soon to begin,
Nerves taut and ready,
Into the arena
I slowly advance

Blood red battle about to begin[6]

BOY!

The mouse clicked
The keyboard tapped
And a web site flashed onto the screen.
Present was a forum with one thousand conflicting opinions and
Boy, what trouble it caused![7]

---

[6] This piece was written on Saturday, February 15th 2003. Its theme is the need to be well prepared for any future conflict.
[7] This piece was written at a student's house on Friday, 18th June 2004. Its theme is the way the Internet can draw one into unexpected conflict.

BRITISH CREED

We believe in god the father of materialism;
Maker of pubs and clubs
And creator of many a good time

We believe in one Lord of pleasure
His only true love child
Everyone's best mate
The life and soul of every party
Who was conceived out of wedlock
Whilst the father was blind drunk

Born of a promiscuous woman
During the 1960s
Prospered under Queen Elizabeth,
Was found stoned and paralytic
Lying in a gutter

He descended into prison
Before being released on bail

He ascended into a perpetual narcotic high
Where he sits and makes merry beside his father.
He keeps on coming back,
To entertain fun lovers everywhere
Whilst not making any value judgments

We believe in the joy of cheap lager
The Lord and giver of pleasure
Who, with the father and the son
Entertains and amuses
Helping us to live only for the moment

We believe in the free spending church of consumerism
With its endless shopping malls;
And ringing, electronic tills

We believe in the importance of money
The fellowship of football
And the joy of getting plastered
Whilst being immersed in many sexual encounters

We look forward to spending many happy hours
Having a good time
In a state of blissful unreality[8]

---

[8] This secular creed was written at a student's house on Wednesday, 16th June 2004. It provides a satirical summary of the bankrupt values of British popular culture.

BULLET

Crack!

I am bullet
A sinister, sliver of metal
A hit man's willing slave
I zip through the air
At merciless speed
A bearer of death
Racing to my target

Thud!

Mission accomplished
A life snuffed out.[9]

---

[9] This meditation was written on Saturday, 27th May 2005. Its theme is the cold, clinical way of killing another human being.

BUTTERFLY BLAIR

I am butterfly Blair
With my fixed grin stare
I enjoy enraging Chancellor Slug Brown
Seeing his green-eyed face creased in a frown
With my gorgeous pink wings
I'm free to do so many things
Soaring up into the sky
Forever on a warm high
I flutter and I flitter
Whilst my critics fuss and twitter,
High in the clouds I spin round and round
Whilst Slug Brown languishes on the ground

I skip prettily from flower to flower
Whilst all my enemies sulk and glower
A most rare species of butterfly am I
Oh Cherie, give me that adoring sigh!
I live in a world of make-believe
My intention of course is NEVER to deceive
Up in the air I giddily soar
Will slug Brown's face ever thaw?
A regular sort of butterfly am I
How in love with myself, oh my!
How happily I twirl round and round

Why slug Brown!
Despite being Prime Minister
You're still on the ground![10]

---

[10] This satirical poem, written on Saturday, January 22nd 2005 (and updated on Saturday 26th April 2008) refers to Prime Minister Tony Blair's troubled relationship with his Chancellor, Gordon Brown. Its theme is the narcissistic self-love of a senior political leader

CAFÉ PIANCO

There is a Café called Pianco
Where hot chocolate is served with marsh-mallow

A picture of Buster Keaton is hung on the wall
It somehow makes him look far too tall
As a place it has only limited space
But wine is served at a cracking pace

On Saturday night the poets crowd in
To make their usual rhyming din
Tea cups rattle
As the poets do battle
To convey their meaning
Amidst the coffee cups steaming

The atmosphere's friendly
Not all the verses are deadly
Soft guitar music gently playing
Male musician slightly swaying

Welcome to Café Pianco
Where hot chocolate is served with marsh-mallow[11]

---

[11] This poem was written late in the evening of Thursday, 20th March 2008. It first emerged whilst the writer was swimming at a local Leisure Centre.

CAREERIST POET

A *'B*****' this'* or an *'F*** that'*
An 'Oh S***' here or a *'you W*****'* there,
Endless obscenities fall from my pen
But why not,
As long as I get my poem published in 'C***' magazine?

Appear *'stoned'* at a major literary festival,
Throw obscenities at a prominent writer
Knock my mistress about
(Better still if she *'tops'* herself)
But why not,
As long as I get that lucrative publishing deal?

Pose as a trendy radical,
Say something offensive in that TV review
Provoke comment from weary critics on *'News Night Review'*
But why not
As long as I get my poetry to sell?

Write a fantasy autobiography about an abused childhood
Put in plenty of sex and violence
My dead parents can't sue for libel
But why not
As long as I attract public attention?

Hang around for long enough
Attend the right political party functions
Be seen with a future Prime Minister
But why not
As long as I get to be a respected poet laureate?
It doesn't matter that I have no talent[12]

---

[12] This monologue was written on Sunday, 3rd February 2008. It expresses the frustration felt by the writer after having read through a poetry booklet which had contained little more than tedious expletives.

CHRISTMAS PLEASURES

Christmas!
Merry, merry Christmas

A season of false cheer
A season of flowing beer
A season of all that's very dear

Christmas!
Merry, merry Christmas

O what joys you offer
Unwanted presents
Unwanted relatives
Unwanted visitors

Christmas!
Merry, merry Christmas

It's time to over-eat
It's time to over-drink
It's time to over-sleep

Christmas!
Merry, merry Christmas

O what peace you give
Rows over the cooking
Rows over the meal
Rows over the dishes

Christmas!
Merry, merry Christmas

Mind numbing gossip
Mind numbing games
Mind numbing television

Turn off the Queen's speech you ******

Christmas!
Merry, miserable Christmas

O what pleasures you leave
Sickly company
Sickly food
Sickly hangovers

Christmas!
Miserable, merry Christmas

Burnt pans to clean
Burnt pudding to bin
Burnt fingers to heal

Christmas!
Miserable, miserable Christmas

Come to a close
Come to an end
Come to a finish –
You season of counterfeit joy[13]

---

[13] This poem was written on Wednesday, 24th November 2004. Its theme is the misery of Christmas.

CLICK!

(How *not* to do Family History Research)

'Click!'
How on earth does this confounded device work?

'Click!'
My wife would insist that I use her new digital camera

'Click!'
Said I needed to find out how it worked

'Click!'
Was always hopeless with these gadgets

'Click!'
Had got it for her birthday; asked me to take good care of it

'Click!'
Drat! I've taken a photo of the pavement

'Click!'
Now, where's that address where my Grandmother was born?

'Click!'
Damn! It's been demolished and replaced by a massage parlour

'Click!'
I don't like the look of that skinhead coming to me with his Alsatian

'Click!'
'Wood! Woof! Woof! Growl! Snarl! Growl!'

'Click!'
Down boy! Down! Is that dog yours sir?

'Click!'
No, I'm not the police; I'm just doing family history!'

'Click!'
Now off to that other address to see if my Great Grandfather's house is still up

'Click!'
Blast! I've just missed the bus

'Click!'
Got here at last! Good, the house is still up… I'll just take one…

'Click!'
'Honk, honk' Yes I was standing in the middle of the road but there's no need to swear

'Click!'
Oh no! That Double Decker bus just got in the way!

'Click!'
Now for the house where my maternal Great, Great Grandparents lived

'Click!'
Drat, it's covered with scaffolding; can't see a thing; one shot will have to do

'Click!'
'Beep, beep' sorry sir, thought this was just a side alley I was standing in

'Click!'
I can't believe it! I've just missed my second bus! I'll have to walk to that Archive Centre

'Click!'
Got to hand my rucksack into security – it's only got some papers in it – oh very well then

'Click!'
What do you mean you don't have the documents – you charged £35.00 for the search!

'Click!'
Try the metropolitan library – but they said you had the documents!

'Click!'
What a waste of time that was! I'll take a photograph of that old Victorian railway station

'Click!'
Honestly constable, doing nothing nefarious, it's just family history

'Click!'
"*A likely story*" you say, well here are the documents to prove it

'Click!'
Do I look like I'm on a terrorist reconnaissance!!!

'Click!'
Thank you constable, 'yes,' I'll be more careful next time

'Click!'
That's all I need, oh no – it's beginning to pour down!

'Click!'
I'm getting soaking wet, I'll nip into that transport café to dry out

'Click!'
Yes, madam, I've been here half an hour and had only one cup of tea

'Click'
No, wasn't suggesting that the milk was off or the buns were stale

'Click!'
Other customers want my place? OK I'll go

'Click!'
The park loo is closed due to vandalism; I'll find somewhere else

'Click!'
Oh nooo! I've put my foot in some dog dirt!

'Click!'
It's bucketing down again and I'm getting s, s, soaking wet

'Click!'
Just that graveyard to see, then I'm off

'Click!'
No, that's not the grave, it must be the one behind all those tall nettles

'Click!'
Ow! Aargh! Eee! These nettles don't half sting! The things I do for my ancestors!

'Click!'
Can barely read the name – it's…

'Click!'
'Aarrrgh!!!' I'm slip---ping on some damp grass

'Click!'
I've landed in some mud and my camera has gone hurtling…

'Click!'
Towards a deep puddle…

'Click!'
'Splat!'

'Click!'
Oh no!

'Click!'
What a day!

'Click!'
Things certainly haven't *'clicked'* with me

'Click!'[14]

CLIMATE CHANGE

See the dreary parched landscape
Desolate of any life

Hear the crackle of an all-consuming fire
As buildings and fields are engulfed

Taste the gritty dust
Stinging on the tongue

Yell with the searing pain
Of glowing red cinders
As they settle on fire-dried skin

Shake with terror at
The bubbling menace of a lifeless sea
Whose aeon-trapped methane belches to the surface

Stare transfixed with bloodshot eyes
At the self-inflicted extinction of
The human race[15]

---

[14] An exaggerated version of the writer's misadventures with his wife's digital camera; he was engaged in family history research at various locations in London (from Thursday 4th-Friday 5th September 2008). It was first performed as an impromptu recital at a community poetry event on Friday, 12th September 2008 and was written down the very next day.

[15] This meditation was written on Friday, 24th August 2007 in a holiday flat at Penzance, Cornwall. It expresses the foreboding felt by the writer at the possibility of climate change.

DAMN THE CRITICS

Am I to be creative?
Too pretentious

Am I to be conventional?
Too pedestrian

Can I write about the present?
Too modern

Can I write about the past?
Too archaic

Could I write on a pastoral theme?
Too boring

Could I write on an urban matter?
Too tedious

Dare I write pure fantasy?
Too obscure

Dare I write gritty realism?
Too depressing

May I write about strong passion?
Too dark

May I write about abstract ideas?
Too intellectual

Might I write in neat verse?
Too formal

Might I write in free-form?
Too fluid

Need I use regular rhyme?
Too forced

Need I use no rhyme?
Too undisciplined

Should I employ striking imagery?
Too distracting

Should I employ plain description?
Too unimaginative

Will I use an elaborate style?
Too contrived

Will I use a simple style?
Too superficial

Would a humorous stance be best?
Too flippant

Would a serious one do?
Too pompous

Alas, what can I do?
Just damn the critics and write![16]

---

[16] This poem was written on Monday, 13th June 2005. Its theme is the sheer frustration of writing poetry.

DENIAL

I just don't know what to do
My partner left me today
My mind whirls in dismay

I really am at a loss
Who will cook for me?
Who will clean for me?

I am utterly upset
There's no one to shout at
There's no one to criticise

I really cannot cope
No one is around to help
No one is around to blame

I just cannot explain
Why she left me
Why she walked out on me

I really was easy to live with[17]

---

[17] This meditation was written on Sunday, 3rd February 2008. It expresses the self-deception which may lie behind a broken relationship.

DRINK

Drink in this lovely view
And let your mind relax

Drink in the lush green fields
Bordered by thin, pencil line walls

Drink in the meandering line of riverside trees
And the scattered patches of deep green woodland

Drink in the toy like, red-roofed houses
Huddled in valley floor intimacy
Drink in the many distant motor vehicles
Parading like multi-coloured ants

Drink in the silently moving goods train
As it glides over a gently curving bridge

Drink in the haze-shrouded ridges
Lying pinioned on a far distant horizon

Drink in a gloriously fertile landscape
Yet to be tanned by a skin burning sun

Drink in everything you see and
Relish the mental peace it brings[18]

---

[18] This poem was written on a scorching day on Ilkley Moor during Tuesday, 2nd June 2009. At the time I was sitting on some rocks overlooking Guiseley. The weather was so hot that I ended-up being sun burned on my arms and legs.

ENTANGLEMENTS

There are three types of men
A single woman should avoid
The *'dead loss dropout'* who never wants to work
The *'depressive inadequate'* wanting to marry *'mummy'* and
The *'dodgy charmer'* with many secrets to hide

There are three types of women
A single man should avoid
The *'desperate predator,'* looking for a perfect *'Mr Right'*
The *'distracted scatter brain'* with endless problems and
The *'divorcee'* with a brood of unruly children

Better to stay single,
With a cup of Bovril in one's hand![19]

---

[19] This poem was written on Saturday, 1st January 2005 after a light-hearted discussion about relationships between myself, my wife and two family friends (mature single ladies) who'd been invited to see the New Year in with us. Its theme is the need to avoid unhealthy entanglements.

EXAM FATIGUE

Yaaaawn!
I am tired
So tired
So very, very tired

Words fumble around
My pain seared mind
Pink-white lights perform
A migraine ballet
Before my eyes,
An iron clamp has been screwed
To rack
The tortured muscles
Of my head

Rushes of anxiety
Shiver up my spine
Driving my heart into
A frantic beat
Unfulfilled deadlines
Provoke a nauseous
Kind of giddiness

Oh, how I long to escape
All of these pressures
By taking a relaxing stroll
In open countryside
Forgetting everything
Out upon wide moorland spaces
Where I can feel as free
As the birds flying above me[20]

---

[20] This piece was written on Saturday, 15th May 2004 and amended on Tuesday, 14th June 2005. Its theme is the incapacitating effects of exam fatigue.

FAME TRAIN

The fame train
Is coming
Hurrying, hurtling
Through a bleak industrial wasteland
Inhabited by sullen, impoverished people
With no hope of a future

The fame train
Is coming
Roaring, rumbling
Through a grimy grey vista
Of blackened back-to-back houses
Lining up steep valley sides

The fame train
Is coming
Whistling, whooping
Through a landscape
Of silent, closed mines
And empty blast furnaces
Where fingers of flame
Once jabbed the air

The fame train
Is coming
Screeching, squealing
To a halt in a large City Centre Station
Whose location could be anywhere?

The fame train
Has arrived
Expectant, waiting
Is it one to board?
Or
Will it run out of control?[21]

---

[21] This poem, written on Friday, 31st December 2004 came clearly to mind whilst walking around the ruins of Kirkstall Abbey, Leeds. Its theme is the way man-made objects like a train, can be used as a metaphor for fame.

FAMILY POLITICS

Shhh!
We don't talk *'politics'* in this family

My wife is a Trade Union representative
Campaigning for fair pay in the Public Sector
She hates the Prime Minister

My eldest son is a cynical Liberal Democrat
He hates the Prime Minister

My middle son is an angry anarchist
He hates the Prime Minister

My youngest son is a Young Conservative
He hates the Prime Minister

My brother is a Telegraph-reading Tory
He hates the Prime Minister

My brother-in-law is a Daily Mirror reading socialist
He hates the Prime Minister

My sister is of the 'plague on all their houses' party
She hates the Prime Minister

My mother is an apolitical pensioner
She hates the Prime Minister

As for my own loyalties?

Shhh!
We don't talk *'politics'* in this family[22]

---

[22] This poem was written on Monday, 29th September 2008.

FLASH, CRASH, DASH

Part 1

Flash! Crash!
A distant rumble
Of thunder
Echoes over
A darkening
Moorland horizon

Flash! Crash!
A nearer rumble
Of thunder
Reverberates
Over a bleak
Moorland ridge

Flash! Crash!
An even closer rumble
Of thunder
Booms over
Steep-sided
Seaside cliffs

Flash! Crash!
Pink sheet
Lightning flickers
In a
Heavy, sweltering
Grey sky

Flash! Crash!
Jagged forked
Lightning shoots
Earthward from
Billowing
Cotton-wool clouds

Part 2

Flash! Crash!
Time for us
Two cliff path
Walkers to
Hurry along

Flash! Crash!
Forked lightning
Performs a
Dancing display,
Time to
Find shelter

Flash! Crash!
Rush! Dash!
Manic panic!
Oh, help!
The storm
Draws near

Flash! Crash!
Rush! Dash!
Manic panic
Rumble! Grumble!
Nerves crumble!
Hurry! Scurry!

Flash! Crash!
Rush! Dash!
Swiftly clambering
Wooden styles,
Breathless, panting,
Heaving, sweating

Part 3

Flash! Crash!
Rush! Dash!
Rasping! Panting!
Heavy rucksack
Slows my
Desperate pace

Flash! Crash!
Near safety
Must get...
Flash! Crash!
That was
Too near!

Flash! Crash!
My wife's ahead
Will... Flash!
Reach... Crash!
The safety
Of the...

Flash! Crash!
Must make...
Flash! Flicker
It! Flash!
Booming Crash!
Dear Lord

Flash! Crash!
She's made it
Thank God
Flash!
Deafening crash!
It's raining

Close

Phew!
Made it
To Flash!
Crash! Safety
Flash! Crash!
CRAAASH!!!
Pop!
The lights
In a
Caravan Park
Launderette
Suddenly
Go out.[23]

---

[23] This poem was written on Saturday, 25th June 2005. It was based upon an incident where my wife and I were caught out in an electrical storm as we walked back along the cliff top from Robin Hood's Bay to Whitby, during the early evening of Sunday, 19th June 2005. Its theme is the drama of being caught out in a severe storm. For further details, please refer to my wife's account of this incident in *'Whitby Storm'* in **Part D** of this book.

FROM HERE I BEGIN

From here I begin
To create and generate

From here I begin
To expand and explore

From here I begin
To reach out and conquer

From here I begin
To follow a lifetime's call[24]

GENOCIDE

One arrest
One cattle truck
One walk to the showers
One death
One out of six million[25]

GENTLE FIRE

How can I make you happy?
Is it possible to fulfil your longings?
What is the best way to please you?
Answers to these questions elude me because a woman's love
Is like a gentle fire –
Warm, snug and dangerous[26]

---

[24] This meditation was originally written in January 1975 when the author had intimations of a possible talent in poetry. The original copy was accidently thrown away in March 1977 and was rewritten from memory on Wednesday, 13th October 2004.

[25] This poem was written on Tuesday, 1st February 2005 – just after the sixtieth anniversary of the liberation of Auschwitz death camp. It is dedicated to the memory of my late father's wartime *'pals'* who sacrificed their lives to defend this country from the evil described here. Its theme is the stark and cold nature of evil.

[26] This meditation was written on Wednesday, 13th September 2006 in response to a persistent request from my wife to leave her a little present under the pillow. It expresses the bewilderment a husband can feel about the complexity of his wife's love.

GIRL WITH A BROKEN SOUL

What are your
thoughts?
What are your
dreams?
Why that far-away
look?
Why that drug-slurred
voice?
All is not what it
seems

Who can repair your
mind?
Who can heal your
heart?
Who can restore your
senses?
Who can show you
love?

Alas not I
Girl with a broken
soul[27]

---

[27] This piece was written on Saturday, 27th May 2005, based upon memories of a poem the writer had first drafted in February 1975. Its theme is the tragedy of mental illness, especially in a young person.

GLACIER

With cold horrific beauty
The glacier grinds relentlessly forward
Inch by crushing inch
Foot by crushing foot
Yard by crushing yard,
King of the ice age
Flanked by a retinue
Of snow covered pinnacles
A white creased robe of ice
Grumbling and groaning along a gouged out valley
(The legacy of a previous ice age)

An irresistible force
Meeting no invincible object

Climate right for it to grow many miles longer
A frozen pitiless majesty
Enough to freeze the heart of any man
Crunching and grinding down the valley
Nothing can halt its stately progress
Rocks, hillocks, the odd withered tree
All consumed by this chill morloch of the soul
Splendid when viewed from afar
Impressive under a halo of bright dawn sunlight
Eerily captivating when seen through a swirl of mist
Pushing and shoving down the gouged out valley
Nothing can withstand its ceaseless advance

A peaceful, sun-swept vista it provides
But the glacier's beauty is of a desolating kind[28]

---

[28] This piece was written on Monday, February 17th 2003. The scene is Snowdonia around 20,000 BC at the height of the last Ice Age. Its theme is the desolating ferocity seen in much of nature.

GLAD TO SEE YOU GO

Goodbye and farewell
Glad to see you go!

Goodbye and farewell
Got you out of my life!

Goodbye and farewell
Good riddance to your snares!

Goodbye and farewell
You can no longer deceive me!

Goodbye and farewell
Your bullying threats are now irrelevant!

Goodbye and farewell
Your manipulative deceits I truly despise!

Goodbye and farewell
Our separation is now complete!

Goodbye and farewell
Your titanium grip has been smashed to pieces!

Goodbye and farewell
A great work of deliverance has taken place!

Goodbye and farewell
I'm now free by God's mercy!

Goodbye and farewell
Phew, I can start anew!

Goodbye and farewell
I am filled with awe at what has been done[29]

---

[29] This piece was written Wednesday, May 28th 2003, whilst recalling at the relief felt following a departure from a bad religious influence in late December 1997.

GOAL!

Older son has got the ball
Younger son takes a tumble
Panting, out of breath father can't keep up
Older son moves forward
It is going to be?
YES, it's a goooooal!
Score; older son one
Panting father nil

Father kicks the plastic ball
Younger son attempts a tackle
Younger son tumbles in the grass
But panting father loses the ball
Older son attempts another strike
Whilst younger son takes another tumble
Older son about to strike
Panting father has lost his breath
Is it going to be?
YES, it's a goooooal!
Most decisive match this
Score; older son two,
Panting father nil

Game now over
Older son smirks in glee
Younger son still rolling on the ground
Panting father staggers to regain his breath
This is *'A. Nobody'*
Reporting on a most exciting match
In the Smith family cup final.[30]

---

[30] This piece was written on Tuesday, April 21st 1992, whilst recalling a football match played with my two younger sons on the field behind the playground at Woodhouse Moor, Leeds. It took place during a warm evening on Easter Sunday, April 19th 1992. They were aged six and nearly four at the time. Its theme is the fun times enjoyed in family life.

GOODBYE, MR GUFF

Farewell, my furry friend
Let me nuzzle you for one last time

Farewell, my furry friend
Allow me to kiss your little head before I go

Farewell, my furry friend
A tear drops from my eyes as I see you waste away

Farewell, my furry friend
Why gaze at me with yellow jaundiced eyes?

Farewell, my furry friend
There's nothing I can do but give you my love

Farewell, my furry friend
Your long silver whiskers droop like a flag at half-mast

Farewell, my furry friend
Your slowly ebbing purr tells of a slowly ebbing life

Farewell, my furry friend
Must dash, a tooth needs filling, wish I could stay

Farewell, my furry friend
Skittish clown of the family, our fond delight

Farewell, my furry friend
So dammed unfair to see you go, aged only two-and a half

Farewell, my furry friend
Why plead with your eyes, we both know it's the end?

Farewell, my furry friend
Crouched on a yellow blanket, awaiting *'Nature's call'*

Farewell, my furry friend
With eyes wide open you sadly beg

Farewell, my furry friend
How can I explain to you there's nothing we can do?

Farewell, my furry friend
You're going to be greatly missed but thanks for being in our lives

Farewell, my furry friend
Missy and Holly will roam the house but you won't be there

Farewell, my furry friend
You've been a wonderful dear pet but now it's a one way trip to the vet

So goodbye, Mr Guff
May we see you again when all things are made new?[31]

GONE!

All this pride
All this profit
All this power
Will be brought to nothing

Soon…

It will all be gone[32]

---

[31] This piece was written in an academic library on Friday, February 14th 2003. It looks back to the time when our second cat *'Mr Guff'* had to be humanely put to sleep on Tuesday, January 28th 2003 having suffered from feline aids. The words *'Farewell, my furry friend'* were the last ones said to him as the writer hurried out for a dental appointment. *'Mr Guff'* had been our pet since Sunday, November 18th 2001. The writer's middle son had suggested the name because Guff had looked *'freaky,'* (and had smelt *'whiffy'* – *'guff'* being the colloquial word for *'breaking wind'*). The poem's theme is the helplessness felt when seeing a well-loved pet slowly die.

[32] This poem first came to mind whilst walking from Baker Street Tube Station on Thursday, 4th September 2008. I had been engaged in family history research in Clerkenwell (and visiting the Hadrian Exhibition held in the British Museum) at the time. Whilst walking, I was gazing at the impressive buildings in the area. Less than two weeks later, in that same vicinity, a major *'meltdown'* of the Global Banking system would begin to take place.

GREEN AND PLEASANT LAND

How pretty are the grassy fields
Of England's green and pleasant land, gently rolling next to
Boarded up houses where loutish youths in base-ball caps roam

How delightful is the ridge woodland
Where lush leaves and yellow blossom
Overhang litter strewn, muddy pathways

How fetching is the fast-flowing beck
Deeply snuggled in its steep valley bottom
Festooned with abandoned cars and shopping trolleys

How sweetly the birds twitter
With melodic song, soothing one's ears until
Suddenly startled by the sound of revving motor cycles

How fragrant is the wildflower
Its scent delightful and delicate
Obliterated by the stench of a nearby leatherworks plant

How softly the bushy undergrowth rubs against my legs
The overhanging foliage gently tapping my forehead
'Ow!' a jagged piece of broken glass has just pierced my shoe

How succulent will the ripening raspberries taste
When, in high summer their contamination gives nothing
But stomach cramps and watery diarrhoea

How quickly the yonder grey squirrel
Leaps from branch to branch, a quivering blur of fur
Terrified by the bark of an uncontrolled Alsatian dog

How charming are my fellow nature lovers
Who, in the vigorous prime of youth, roam around with
Shaven heads, tattooed arms and head crunching boots

How nice it is to celebrate England's rural idyll
In a beautiful, lush green landscape, nestling against
Vistas of high-rise flats and sink-slum Council Estates[33]

HAY FEVER MISERY

Achooo! Sniffle, sneeze, snort
Awaken early to a morning fever and discordant broken poetry

Achooo! Sniffle, sneeze, snort
The misery season has begun

Achooo! Sniffle, sneeze, snort
Got forty days more of this

Achooo! Sniffle, sneeze, snort
Everything around me is a watery blur

Achooo! Sniffle, sneeze, snort
My ears are clogged up with a soft squelchy wax

Achooo! Sniffle, sneeze, snort
My nose discharges a silvery, slippery mucus

Achooo! Sniffle, sneeze, snort
My tongue can only taste a thick, yellow phlegm

Achooo! Sniffle, sneeze, snort
My skin prickles with a red, ruddy rash

Achooo! Sniffle, sneeze, snort
My breath comes out as a strangulated wheeze

Achooo! Sniffle, sneeze, snort
My disordered bladder constantly springs a leak

---

[33] This meditation was written on Monday, 31st May 2004, whilst walking on Meanwood Ridge, Leeds, looking towards Scott Hall Bank. Its theme is the way human beings can easily despoil the countryside.

Achooo! Sniffle, sneeze, snort
Strength drains away, yet I cannot sleep

Achooo! Sniffle, sneeze, snort
Everyone, everywhere in every situation annoys me

Achooo! Sniffle, sneeze, snort
I dread newly cut grass, I dread exhaust fumes, I dread any smoke

Achooo! Sniffle, sneeze, snort
I hate the world, I hate people, I hate you all

Achooo! Sniffle, sneeze, snort
I just want to lash out at all who get in my way

Achooo! Sniffle, sneeze, snort
I shout at my wife, I shout at the cat, I shout at the air

Achooo! Sniffle, sneeze, snort
I loathe those who burden me with their problems

Achooo! Sniffle, sneeze, snort
I couldn't give a damn about others

Achooo! Sniffle, sneeze, snort
People look on in disgust when I sneeze out a watery shrapnel

Achooo! Sniffle, sneeze, snort
No one understands, no one cares, no one shows any sympathy

Achooo! Sniffle, sneeze, snort
Got to skulk indoors; a refuge from the sun

Achooo! Sniffle, sneeze, snort
Must take frequent baths to soothe my scabby skin

Achooo! Sniffle, sneeze, snort
Almost deaf, I feel like death cooled down

Achooo! Sniffle, sneeze, snort
How long will this watery purgatory last?

Achooo! Sniffle, sneeze, snort
Can there ever be any joy in this?

Achooo! Sniffle, sneeze, snort
Ah yes, just one joy – the ability to inflict my misery upon others

HIGHLAND VISTA

White topped mountain,
Towers above white topped mountain,
Like frozen waves in an icy sea;

Ice covered pinnacle
Soars above ice covered pinnacle
Like the stakes of a high security fence;

A cruel, cold, clammy wind whistles a forlorn tune
Over boggy, barren covered plateaus;
Gusts of roaring, rushing air flows across
Empty, bracken covered moors;

Sheer rocky sides veer down
To a loch of black shimmering water:
Steep debris strewn slopes descend toward
A marshy glen bottom, crossed by a narrow sandstone path;

In the near distance green pine covered hills,
In the far distance a relentless array of mountains.
A setting both to impress and depress

See the wild life flee
The latest invasion band of tourists
All trudging up a narrow stone-strewn path;

Hear a distant bird's warning cry,
Panicked by a global army of visitors
Sweating in their garish, gaudy cagoules

Smell the musty, herbal odour of
Many different plants;

Feel the relentless ache in their muscle stretched limbs
As they slowly place one foot after another
Relentlessly aiming for a mountain peak
Made a place of mystery by a swirling mist

Taste the delightful sweetness of cool orange liquid
Gulped down by a dry, arid throat
Desperate for any liquid refreshment

A quiet curse for those tourists whose cigarette smoke
Swirls back onto the faces of those
Panting and heaving behind them

Why do they come?
What are they here for?
Why the self-inflicted torment?
Is it the challenge?
Is it the escape?
Is it simple curiosity?
Or the desire to personally experience the rugged vista
That is Highland Scotland?[34]

---

[34] This meditation was written on Tuesday, 24th August 2004, at Pitlochry, Scotland. Its theme is the puzzlement felt over the way people willingly endure great discomfort in order to enjoy spectacular scenery.

HOUSE, MOUSE, ROUSE

Mouse, mouse
In the house
Scurrying along the kitchen floor

Screaming, terrified wife,
In fear of her life
With mad-eyed stare
Balancing on a wobbling wooden chair

*"Hit it with a frying pan!
Hit it with a frying pan!"*

Bang!
Bang!
Bang!

"Damn! I missed!"

"You're useless!"

Bang!
Bang!
Bang!

"It's too quick my dear!"

*"Chuck in the cat!
Chuck in the cat!
Never mind if she's a bit fat!"*

Cat chucked in
She emits a protesting meow

(Half an hour later)

Slowly open the kitchen door,
Mouse still scurrying along the floor
Cat asleep on the table top

Oh, what a useless great flop!

*"Drive it out!
Drive it out!"*

"I will, my dear"

*"Make a noise!
Make a noise!"*

"What do you think I'm making!"

"Try the frying pan again!"

Bang!
Bang!
Bang!

Cat hides under the kitchen table
This certainly is no fable
Terrified wife slams the kitchen door

*"Oh no, it's gone in the living room
It's under the bed-settee!"*

*"Drive it out!
Drive it out!"*

"I am trying, my dear"

*"It's no good you just shouting
'Rouse!'
'Rouse!'
'Rouse!'"*

"Try the frying pan again!"

*Bang!
Bang!
Bang!*

One protesting squeak,
A flash of brown rodent fur,
Dramatic exit through the open garden door –
Past the twitching feline nose
Of a big ginger-striped Tom

"Missed that one, it was going so quick"

Terrified wife
Slams the garden door shut
And with wide-eyed look
Stares around

*"There's no mouse in the house
There's no mouse in the house"*

*"It's
Gone!
Gone!
Gone!"*

With red-faced looks
We sink into each other's arms sighing

*'Phew!'
'Phew!'
'Phew!'*[35]

---

[35] This frivolous poem was written on the morning of Sunday, 16th March 2008 and is (with only a little poetical exaggeration) based upon an incident which took place during the summer of 2003.

HURRY! HURRY! HURRY!

(A Poem Dedicated To All Students Bogged Down With Coursework and Exam Pressures)

Hurry, hurry, hurry
Rush, rush, rush,
Busy, busy, busy,
Pressure, pressure, pressure,
Scurry, scurry, scurry,
Plan, plan, plan,
Read, read, read,
Write, write, write,
Headache, headache, headache,

Help! I'm FALLING into a quagmire of endless hard work

Hassle, hassle, hassle
Go! Go! Go!
Bustle, bustle, bustle,
Chase, chase, chase,
Deadline, deadline, deadline,
Revise, revise, revise,
Search, search, search
Study, study, study

Help! I'm SINKING into a quagmire of endless hard work

Fast, fast, fast,
Quick, quick, quick,
Ring, ring, ring,
Answer, answer, answer,
E-mail, e-mail, e-mail
Reply, reply, reply
Exam, exam, exam,
Fail, fail, fail,

Help! I'm DROWNING in a quagmire of endless hard work

Flounder, flounder, flounder,
Under, under, under
Gurgle, gurgle, gurgle
Bubble, bubble, bubble
Deep, deep, deep,
Sleep, sleep, sleep,
Drowned, drowned, drowned,
Dead, dead, dead

Help! I'm BURIED under a quagmire of endless hard work[36]

---

[36] This poem was written on Wednesday, March 21st 1990 whilst under extreme personal pressure on a postgraduate *'Diploma in Management Studies'* Course. It was slightly updated and amended on Thursday, June 4th 2003. Its theme is the sense of exhaustion, when overwhelmed by an endless amount of academic work.

I PROTEST

I protest at the decadence of Post Modern Western Society
I protest at the spread of a cancerous drug culture
I protest at the filth pumped through the media
I protest at the ceaseless mockery of good moral values
I protest at the glorification of violence
I protest at the obscenity masquerading as art
I protest at the mindless cult of celebrity
I protest at the neglect of Inner City areas
I protest at the red tape throttling commercial enterprise
I protest at the *'Fat Cat'* bonuses awarded to failed bankers
I protest at the plight of this or that social group
I protest at the peer pressure to look young and *'cool'*
I protest at the proliferation of useless government jobs
I protest at the breakdown of major Public Organisations
I protest at the inefficiency of our local Town Hall
I protest at the endless *'spin doctoring'* of Politicians
I protest at the unethical Foreign Policy followed by our Government
I protest at the silly hairstyles of our youth
I protest at the growing restriction placed upon individual freedom
I protest at the criminal softness of our Judiciary
I protest at the presence of crooked lawyers
I protest at the deadness of public religion
I protest, because so far I can do so without fear of arrest.[37]

---

[37] This ranting protest was written on Saturday, May 24th 2003. Its theme is the sense of alienation caused by Post-Modern Society. It was updated on Wednesday 31st March 2010 in order to insert a reference to banker bonus payments.

IF MY CAT COULD SPEAK

If my cat could speak
What would she say?

She would tell of her adventures
When chasing birds and mice
And of scraps with
Neighbouring cats,
And how she escaped that 'Tom'
By fleeing onto the ledge of a railway bridge
As a train clattered and rumbled underneath.

If my cat could speak
What would she say?

She would tell of the time she crossed
The busy road outside,
Strolling along
With bushy tail flicking the air
As a metal and glass cage
Screeched noisily to a halt
A man locked inside
Angrily shaking his fist,
And shouting words
(In strange 'human speak,')
Words beginning with
'B' and 'F'

If my cat could speak
What would she say?

She would mention
The midnight cats' *'chorus'*
Of lights flicking on
And of more strange 'human speak'
With words also beginning with
'B' and *'F'*

Best of all she would say: -
'I love you,
Now, where's my food?[38]

---

[38] This meditation was written on Wednesday, 12th December 2007. It expresses the mystique of cats.

IF YOU SAY

RULES FOR HELPING YOUR WIFE TO CHOOSE NEW CLOTHES IN A SHOP

The simplest rule applicable to all men everywhere is **'DON'T!'** Plead a cold, a headache or even say you have the Black Death in order to escape the terrible ordeal of shopping with your wife. Claim you've got to see *'mother,'* the Doctor or even the local MP. Pretend you've got that urgent business trip in Outer Siberia. But if your *'other half'* does blackmail you into accompanying her on a shopping expedition then here are a few rules to limit the damage that will be done to your nerves.

<u>RULE 1:</u> Never expect anything you say to be right when she's trying on some new clothes, for

If you say, *'Darling you look gorgeous'* she'll retort, *'You're being sarcastic.'*

If you say, *'You look quite fetching'* she'll retort, *'You're being insincere.'*

If you say, *'You look nice'* she'll retort, *'You're just trying to fob me off.'*

If you say, *'You should definitely get it'* she'll retort, *'You're being dictatorial.'*

If you say, *'You're best making up your own mind'* she'll retort, *'You don't care.'*

If you say, *'You look OK'* she'll retort, *'You really don't like it.'*

If you say, *'I don't like it'* she'll retort, *'You don't love me anymore.'*

If you say nothing, she'll retort, *'You're not giving a lead.'*

RULE 2: Never expect anything you do to be right when she's trying on some new clothes, for

If you stand around doing nothing, she'll retort, *'You just look gormless.'*

If you look to heaven for inspiration, she'll retort, *'You should be looking at me!'*

If you sigh in exasperation, she'll retort, *'You're being an embarrassment.'*

If you try to hum a jaunty tune, she'll retort, *'You're distracting me.'*

If you sit cross legged on the floor, reading a newspaper, she'll retort, *'You look like a tramp.'*

If you dash outside to read a book she'll drag you back in, saying, *'You're being a disgrace.'*

But remember, the very worst thing to do when she tries on something new is to burst out laughing, at which point she'll burst into tears and give you a good thumping. However, with luck she'll never ever again invite you to help her with clothes shopping.[39]

---

[39] This list of rules was written on Thursday 23rd April 2009 following an exasperating shopping expedition with my wife.

ILKLEY HAIKU 1

Hazy blue sky
Blackened burnt heather
Gentle, rolling moor

Warm wafting breeze
Glacier dumped rocks
Chattering walkers

Treacherous bog land
Old stone circles
Scattered flock

An ant procession
Marches beneath a rock
In neat parade

Lone bird cry
As it flies overhead
Above a ridge

Ilkey Moor
September Eleven
Twenty O Six

Five years after a war began[40]

---

[40] This haiku poem was written whilst seated on a large grey rock near the top of Ilkley Moor during the afternoon of Monday, 11th September 2006. The date marked the fifth anniversary of the destruction of the twin towers in New York.

ILKLEY HAIKU 2

Wharfedale Valley
Grey Ilkley settlement
Faint traffic noise

Grey-blue sky
Brown tinted trees
Withering ferns

White bathhouse
Long wooden tables
Resting walkers

Distant owl calling
Buzzing flies swarming
Distant dog barking

Autumn falling
Fading white sunbeam
Late summer's end[41]

---

[41] This haiku poem was written on a slope of Ilkley Moor whilst sitting in the late morning on a large wooden bench by a newly restored bathhouse on Monday, 18th September 2006

ISBN NIGHTMARE

Breathless,
I run, panic-stricken
Across a snowy plain
Ice crunching beneath my boots
Vibrating ISBN Numbers
Bounding along after me

Bang! I'm struck by a **1**
Bash! I'm hit by a **2**
Biff! I'm felled by a **3**

I stagger up and run on

Crash! I'm thumped by a **4**
Crump! I'm floored by a **5**
Thump! I'm kicked by a **6**

I stagger up and run on

Thwack! I'm swiped by a **7**
Whack! I'm knocked by a **8**
Wham! I'm attacked by a **9**

With effort, I regain my feet
And run on toward
Distant snow-capped mountains
Dazzling white against a cloudy grey sky
Swarming and humming with ISBN numbers
I tumble forward
Through an encircling **0**
Only to wake up
Enveloped in a warm, clammy sweat

It's morning and my ISBN nightmare has ended
For now[42]

---

[42] This poem was written on Thursday 9th July 2010 after three gruelling days examining the procedures needed to purchase ISBN numbers for a series of books I was preparing. It had first emerged in visual form during a poetry session the previous evening.

LAND OF PARADOX

America!

Land of iron
Land of clay

Land of success
Land of failure

Land of love
Land of hate

Land of hope
Land of dope

Land of faith
Land of unbelief

Land of Founding Fathers
Land of domineering mothers

Land of the free
Land of the slave

Land of cowboy idealism
Land of Indian extermination

Land of golden dreams
Land of impoverished nightmares

Land of crowded forests
Land of empty plains

Land of shimmering deserts
Land of arctic wastes

Land of towering cities
Land of scattered farms

Land of luxurious hotels
Land of rickety motels

Land of *'Star Trek'*
Land of Shuttle wreck

Land of media glamour
Land of noisy clamour

Land of easy tolerance
Land of racist bigotry

Land of brilliant genius
Land of *'Dumb and Dumber'*

Land of Puritan constraint
Land of no restraint

Land of glitzy cheerleaders
Land of drug-worn prostitutes

Land of ambition
Land of contrition

Land of immense wealth
Land of ill health

Land of big business
Land of *'monkey business'*

Land of rare financial success
Land of common financial failure

Land of the baseball team
Land of the ghetto gang

Land of rigid law and order
Land of indiscriminate shooting

Land of flamboyant individuality
Land of harsh conformity

Land of endless life stories
Land of many brooding silences

Land of honest openness
Land of sinister secrets

Land of loud, spontaneous guffaws
Land of cold, conspiratorial calculation

Land of abundant opportunity
Land of restricting snobbery

Land of great political power
Land of timid craven fear

Land of keen government debate
Land of the FBI and the CIA

Land of gleaming technology
Land of dodgy theology

Land of many Churches
Land of countless bars

Land of fervent piety
Land of casual blasphemy

America!

Land of paradox
Land of contradiction

One nation or many –
What is America?[43]

---

[43] This piece was written at Chorlton Street Bus Station, Manchester on Thursday, June 5th 2003. Its theme is the many contradictions of American Society.

LAST HOLIDAY WITH MY YOUNGEST SON

A feeling of sadness
A feeling of sorrow
That I didn't spend more time
With my children when they were young

A sense of regret
A sense of relief
That this has been our last
Holiday together as father and son

Time to let go
Time to leave you
Before the carriage door closes on your
Smirking boyish face, with its look of heartfelt relief

A thunderclap roar
A clattering rumble
As your train heaves out of Berwick, leaving
Me alone on a platform
With a head full of brooding memories[44]

---

[44] This meditation was written on Sunday, 22nd August 2004. It was based upon an incident at Berwick-Upon-Tweed Railway Station during the previous Wednesday, when I'd left the train, leaving my youngest son (aged sixteen years) to continue his journey alone to Leeds. From Friday, 13th August, we'd been holidaying together in Seahouses and Edinburgh. (In actual fact, we were to enjoy one more holiday together before he left home in Aberdeen, Scotland. This was two years later – the time he received his 'A' Level results.)

LEEDS LOUTS

Ayup,
Loutish lads
Eating well at
Eddy's stag do
Drinking heavily
Soon fighting with chairs and broken beer glasses

Lager swilling
Ogling
Unpleasant
Tykes[45]
Spewing vomit as they stagger into the street[46]

LOVE FEVER

How can I express my love for you
My sweetheart?

How can I repay your loving kindness
My friend?

How can I probe the mystery of our love
My dearest?

Poetry can't do it
Prose can't do it
Praise can't do it

Better to end my love-sick prattle
And give you
My all instead[47]

---

[45] A Yorkshire term for *'type'*
[46] This acrostic poem was first written on Friday, 9th October 2009
[47] This poem was written on Wednesday, 22nd June 2005 in the bedroom of our Guest House in Beverley, East Yorkshire. Its theme is the way we can still be lost for words when in love.

LOVELY LIZARD

Lovely-lovely Lizard
Lovely-lovely fields
Lovely-lovely cliffs
Watch the bobbing seals

Come! Visit
Britain's southernmost point
A triangle of defiance
Jutting out into the Sea

Lovely-lovely Lizard
Lovely-lovely fields
Lovely-lovely cliffs
Watch the bobbing seals

Come! Visit
This bastion against stormy waters
Boldly defying the waves
Holding back the tides

Lovely-lovely Lizard
Lovely-lovely fields
Lovely-lovely cliffs
Watch the bobbing seals

Come! Visit
A sanctuary for many birds and insects
A shelter for many psychedelic flowers
A *'must see'* for many hikers

Lovely-lovely Lizard
Lovely-lovely fields
Lovely-lovely cliffs
Watch the bobbing seals

Come! Visit
The last rocks of England
Gasp at breathtaking views
Relax under a warm Cornish sunlight

Lovely-lovely Lizard
Lovely-lovely fields
Lovely-lovely cliffs
Watch the bobbing seals

Come! Visit
England's southernmost Church
Stroll up a narrow cove pathway
Enjoy the tea and scones kindly laid on

Lovely-lovely Lizard
Lovely-lovely fields
Lovely-lovely cliffs
Watch the bobbing seals [48]

---

[48] This poem was written on Saturday, 3rd July 2010 whilst reminiscing about a visit made to the Lizard (in Southern Cornwall) during August 2007 and 2008.

LOVELY WIFE

You are my lovely wife
Who shows great patience when I lose things
Cuddly and sweet, you're my perfect companion
I am enthralled by your gentle presence
I adore your quirky little ways

Being married to you is a great privilege
Being your friend is a wonderful thing

How passionately I long to show you my love
But alas, many pressing distractions intrude
I wish there was time to snuggle up to you
But there's not even a chance for a quick kiss

I wish I could think of you more often
But other thoughts crowd into my busy brain
I wish I could lose things less often
But the intensity within my mind distracts me
From life's more mundane things

I wish I could give you the attention you crave for
But a myriad of professional duties call me away

You are so precious to me
That I want to be with you forever
You are so lovely in every way
That you lose me in heartfelt admiration
You are so playful in your manner
That I lighten up with many a smile
You are the very best of women
My love for you increases with age

Let me take time to think of you
So that other thoughts aren't allowed to intrude
Let me be less careless about mislaying things
And focus again upon life's mundane things
So I no longer try your patience

Let me be more attentive about your many anxieties
So you're more able to cope with the pressures of work

How good you are and deserving of my love
I shall put aside my many distracting duties
Taking care to snuggle against your cute little body
Showering you with many kisses

May my love for you continue into old age
May I cease trying your over-stretched patience
May our sweet companionship last forever
May I constantly continue to court and woo you
May I always appreciate your quirky little ways[49]

MADWOMAN

Madwoman, wild eyed stare
Screeching, screaming
Swearing curses, stumbling
Shuffling
Muttering, mumbling
Voices echoing in your head

A rickety park bench
Your only bed
Death head junkies peer and sneer
Adding to your trembling fears

No one cares for you now
Tonight you'll take a final bow
Suddenly, those voices will cease

For tomorrow, you'll be found
Dead –
By the police[50]

---

[49] This poem was written on Wednesday, 21st January 2009. It was produced as a *'peace offering'* to the writer's wife after he'd been in a temper over mislaying his shaving bag.
[50] This meditation was written on Saturday, 27th May 2005 and was based on a poem the writer had first written in August 1976 after listening to a mentally disturbed woman shouting profanities near the Earls Court Road, London. It was heavily revised on Tuesday, 14th June 2005 following the suggestions of another poet and the writer's wife

MATCH STICK LONELINESS

Another desolate scene
Drawn by
A desolate man
Emotionally smothered by a mother's love
Unable to communicate
Except through his art

Match stick men
Matched by
Match stick chimneys
Berwick *'cum'* Salford
All crafted by one man
Experiencing desolate loneliness

The artist *'Lowry'*
Now turned into a tourist attraction
Is this what he would have wished?[51]

---

[51] This meditation was written on Sunday, 22nd August 2004 – the day after my wife and I had completed *The Lowry Walk* around Berwick-upon-Tweed. It explores how a lonely artist can end up serving the tourist industry long after his death.

MATCHING COLOURS

Grey rocks
Grey sheep
Greying sky

Green grass
Green trees
Greening landscape

Grey houses
Grey roads
Greying settlement

Green ferns
Green heather
Greening vista

Two colours dominating
A lush valley view
Seen from a grey-green seat
On the green-grey slope of Ilkley Moor[52]

---

[52] This poem was written on Friday, 4th June at the Addingham end of Ilkely Moor.

MELTDOWN

The world's gone insane
Lusting for financial gain
Investors in pain

Shares lose value
Currencies devalue

Banks cease to trade
As debts cascade
And go unpaid

Executives resign
That's a bad sign

It's come to a head
Panic will spread
There's no bread

City – too much greed
Wealth can't breed

Shares take a massive tumble
Stockbrokers fumble
Apologies they mumble

Assets quickly go
Credit doesn't flow

A crash is here
Bankers quake with fear
Pundits play the seer

Calamity wasn't foreseen
But that's another theme

A new order is born
As many mourn
The goods they pawn

Lots of revulsion
Amidst global convulsion

In this night
No remedy in sight
Reason's taken flight

In a mood of gloom
Economists see doom

It's all very sad
The world's gone mad
People crying...
'We've been had!'[53]

---

[53] This poem was written on Friday, 19th September 2008, whilst seated on some rocks on Ilkley Moor. During the previous Monday, the *'meltdown'* of the Global Financial system had begun to take place when the large investment bank, Lehman Brothers filed for bankruptcy

METRO CLASS-SCAPE

Chiltern countryside
Melts into wealthy country village
Where Rock Stars
In plush mansions live

Wealthy country village
Melts into prosperous outer suburb
Where wealthy stockbrokers
In detached houses live

Prosperous outer suburb
Melts into respectable inner suburb
Where retired professionals
In snug semi's live

Respectable inner suburb
Melts into modern housing estate
Where council workers
In cramped maisonettes live

Modern housing estate
Melts into slum, 'sink' estate
Where asylum seekers
In emergency accommodation cower

Slum, 'sink' estate
Melts into prosperous commercial centre
Where self-made billionaires
In plush penthouses live

Prosperous commercial centre
Melts into a core governing centre
Where shady politicians
In deep corruption walk quickly to and fro[54]

---

[54] This poem was written on Tuesday 22nd September 2009, three days after I'd returned from a family history trip in London. The poem is loosely based upon my view from a train whilst travelling from the outer suburb of Rickmansworth to inner London.

MISDIRECTED COMPLIMENTS

You're beautiful
You're gorgeous
You're lovely –
Clad in that warm fur coat

You're clever
You're nice
You're wonderful
With those beautiful feminine eyes

Ah! Tender feelings you arouse
Mmmm! Let me kiss your head
Rrrr! You're fabulous to be with

Thud! The kitchen door bursts open

Why the misery guilt expression on your face?
Is it because I was talking to the cat and not to you, my dear wife?[55]

---

[55] This piece was written on Thursday, May 29th 2003 and slightly revised on Tuesday, 21st December 2004 in response to criticism from another poet. Its theme is the danger of showing more affection to one's cat than to one's wife.

MISSING MISSY

Goodbye Missy, my furry bundle of love
I will miss all of your feline ways
The way you used to nuzzle me
And lick my hair
Rubbing against my legs
Treating me as if I was your kitten
I will miss your gentle purring
Your look of trusting affection
And the way you used to flick my face
With your big, bushy beaver tail
No longer are you there to greet me
After a hard day's work
Or to amuse me
By lolling around on the bed
As if you owned everything

Yet, despite your last illness
(When your congested lungs laboured to breathe
Amidst a cluster of malignant lumps)
Your life was still a happy one
You were ever the proverbial pampered pussy cat
And even in your last hours
You delighted to sit on your tummy
In the grassed area around the back
Your head nodding up and down
In watchful observation

Now you're gone
Buried by a kind neighbour
Beneath the ground
You loved to play on

Missy,
Our dear *'sweet-pea girl,'*
Our silly *'popsey-wopsey'*
We all miss you
As a cat you were a great pet
A very special part of our family

And it was good to know
That you were still doing *'catty things'* until
The very last hours of your life
And even as death approached
Another cat watchfully circled you around
Protecting you
And showing us where you lay
Dear sweet *'Missy Meow'*
You were a lovely animal
And now our flat
Seems empty and desolate without you
...But thanks for being in our lives[56]

---

[56] This lament was written on Saturday, 28th June 2008, the day after our white tabby cat, Missy, was found dead outside a neighbour's flat door. Aged eight, she had been ill with cancer of the lymph glands since February and had been in our ownership since May 2002. It wasn't until Sunday, 10th January 2010 that we obtained another cat – a neutered male called *'Smitten.'*

MISSY! MISSY!

Part 1

Missy, Missy burning bright
To a bird you're not a pretty sight

Crouched there on a window sill
Faint sweet birdsong *'turns you on'*
Killer instincts now aroused
As the garden your eyes do browse
Tiger tail cuts through the air
Eyes look out with a focused stare
Through a bedroom window you peer
With a look that's ferociously queer
Crouched down wanting to pounce
Garden birds weigh only an ounce
A fat black crow gives a call
You only wish it would fall
White tabby head swings left to right
You are now ready for a fight
Tame pussy you are not
You prowl there on the spot
Whiskers twitch up and down
Upright ears form a pointed crown

Missy, Missy burning bright
You are certainly an impressive sight
I hope the birds soon take flight

Part 2

Missy, Missy burning bright
Your screech echoed through the night

Us humans you kept awake
With the loud din you did make
With Dregs the Tom you did scrap
His tatty fur was very black
From our beds we heard you screech
Dregs you put beyond our reach
Your territory he did invade
But his scent will not pervade
Hunter instincts were at play
Dregs most certainly could not stay
With Holly he did wish to mate
But he had left it far too late
She's now safely in
Away from that infernal din
A rattle of a dustbin lid
Behind the outhouse he's gone and hid
A neutered cat you now are
So with you Dregs can't go too far
Now scratching on the door
You no longer want any more
In the dark I stagger up
Hoping you will shut up
Into the front room you slowly enter
You treat our house as a battlefield centre

Missy, Missy burning bright
Your screech echoed through the night
Our sleep you did blight

Part 3

Missy, Missy sleeping tight
You've been out all night

Curled up on your mat
On which you now lie flat
Feline eyes tightly shut
On your back one slight cut
Fought that Tom you certainly did
Now in our house safely hid
Dreaming of chasing birds and mice
To you it's very nice
Light snore is your only noise
You have assumed a calm restful pose
Stomach now well filled
Wild instincts quietly stilled
Cats have a strange mystique
For dogs it must seem very bleak
Tame pussy you are now
Your head curled in a reverent bow
Lying there very still
Let us worry about the vet's bill

Missy, Missy sleeping tight
You've been out all night
Dregs the stray Tom you put to flight[57]

---

[57] Part One of this early and experimental poem was written on Friday, May 30th 2003, whilst watching our cat scan the garden from a bedroom windowsill; Part Two was initially drafted on Thursday 5th June 2003 and Part Three, the day before. A reading of William Blake's late eighteenth century poem *Tiger Tiger* inspired this poem

MORNING MAIL

Clatter, tumble, drop!
The morning mail has come
(But not *'soft and regular'* or else I'll be sued)

Will it be from the two nice ladies in Surrey with kind messages of support?
Or from that mad man in Belfast who thinks I'm *'The Beast?'*

Will it be from the goofy American gentleman who loves to recount his life story?
(For the umpteenth time!)
Or from that aggressive Texan dame who loves to belittle her husband?
(Also, for the umpteenth time!)

Will it be from that simple man, desperate for a wife?
Or from that frumpy PHD female, desperate for a husband?
(Not me, thank goodness!)

Will it be from a neighbour, asking me to look after her pet?
Or from that window cleaner whose not yet been paid?

Will it be from Uncle Bill as a hastily scrawled one-word post card?
Or from Aunt Agatha announcing one of her *'Queenly'* visits?

Will it be from that charity with its endless appeals for money?
Or from that Competition announcing a glorious big win?

Will it be from the dodgy Finance Company offering free cash?
Or from the Tax Office in the brown, coffin shaped envelope?

Who knows what the Morning Mail may bring?[58]

---

[58] This piece was written on Thursday, May 29th 2003, days after I'd read a poem penned by a certain public figure concerning the large amount of *'hate mail'* he'd received on taking up his position. (A reference is made to it in the third line.) The overarching theme of this poem is the unpredictability of the morning mail.

MULTIPLE-SURRENDER

A slow, meandering river
Surrenders to
Dark green woodland

Dark green woodland
Surrenders to
Lush hillside fields

Lush hillside fields
Surrender to
Steep, dusty moorland

Steep, dusty moorland
Surrenders to
A blue, hazy sky

Blue, hazy sky
Surrenders to
A shining, shimmering sun

A multiple surrender
In a haven of peace[59]

---

[59] This poem was written on Ilkely Moor on Bank Holiday Monday, 25th May 2009. I'd been sitting on some rocks overlooking the Addingham aspect of the Wharfedale valley.

NEWS IMPACT

The news is bad again today
Poetic words can't express my dismay
What can I do or say?

Blood and gore is all I see
On my large-screen colour TV
It's just the same in cyberspace
Wicked cruelty gathers pace
Blood flows in the city
War rages without pity
Hungry crowds mill listlessly round
While children collapse dead to the ground

The whole world has gone mad
It's really getting very bad
Things are not what they seem
Wish it were all a bad dream
About Global warming
We've had enough warning
It's enough to make you cry
As our world begins to boil and fry

Politicians deliver their smooth-tongued patter
Does what they say really matter?
They *'spin'* and lie
As our culture begins to die
Most prefer the Big Brother den
Lots more fun than *'News at Ten'*
Who's left to protest or care?
Life is just so damn unfair

As reason hides in deep sleep at night
An insidious oppression prepares to bite
Stripping each liberty one-by-one
Denying the freedoms our ancestors won

Ssshh!!! Watch out!
The police are about
And prison will serve as your fate
For this country is no longer a free State

After all –
This is an age of red-hot, ice-cold hate[60]

---

[60] This meditation was written on Wednesday, 1st March 2006 and expresses the anxiety created by an endless round of negative news bulletins.

NIGHT WIND

Hear the night wind blow
Hear the night wind blow
Hear it gather strength as it whips across choppy ocean waters
With ships lurching and swaying in its wake
Hear it swirl over a weather-beaten shore
Hear it cross muddy ploughed fields
Hear it push its rain drenching clouds
Over a bleak moorland ridge

Blow, blow mighty shrieking wind!
Pluck the dying leaves from swaying autumn trees and
Throw them near and far in furious whirlwind eddies

Pluck the slates from farmhouse roofs and
SMASH them onto the cobble stoned farmyard below

Pluck the wooden farm gate from its hinges and
THROW it against a dry stone wall

Pluck the scarecrow from the ground and
HURL it into a distant whispering hedgerow

Blow, oh blow, mighty strengthening gale
Blow with a frenzied, awesome fury
Blow you noisy herald of a chill, leaden winter
Tell of snows and floods yet to come
Strike terror into the hearts of proud humanity
Show what a hurricane storm can do

Listen to the cattle lowing in the field
Hear the bleats of frightened sheep
Note how the horses neigh and paw at the ground,
Galloping this way and that in equestrian panic
Even the pigs squeal loudly in protest
From inside a darkened farm kitchen a dog barks wildly
With even the cat sitting upright in its basket
Ears pricked up
Attentive to the howling onrush

CRASH!

A tree is plucked from its roots
And flung onto the ground like a broken match stick

The wind catches overhanging cables
Causing them to emit a high pitched hum

A chain beats against a metal gate post

An old plastic bag
Is blown hither and thither
High, then low then high again

The door of a lonely and abandoned farmhouse
Swings forlornly to and fro
Echoing monotonously through the night
Repeatedly banging, banging, banging
Against its frame

Twigs are torn away
Like human arms in a bomb explosion

Branches bend backward in abject submission
Before the wind's all encompassing majesty

An old television aerial
Tumbles down into a muddy farm yard

Soon to be joined by a fallen chimney pot

Something has smashed through
A greenhouse window

A car is buffeted along
A winding country lane

At sea, waves pile upwards
As if pulled by an invisible hand

Only to disintegrate into a fermenting, foaming fury
As they hurl themselves against a sodden shore

The lighthouse lantern blinks steadily on
Warning the ships of the razor-sharp rocks
Lurking beneath this camouflage
Of white foam

Inside his buffeted outpost
The coastguard looks through
His binoculars
But can see nothing
His radar screen alone tracing the
Forlorn ships trapped by the storm

With a plopping sound
Chunks of muddy cliff
Drop into the churning, seething sea
And the coastline reluctantly retreats once more

The gale continues with an unabated, relentless intensity

Another large wave crashes against the shore

Indoors people huddle in their beds
Waiting anxiously for the storm to pass
Listening with straining ears to every unwarranted noise
A dustbin lid is thrown to the ground

Wooden rafters creak ominously in the wind

CRASH!

Another tree is plucked from its roots
And hits the earth

Outside the temperature falls
As sleeting rain
Ricochets like tiny meteorites off
A tightly closed bedroom window

Puddles grow into pools and then small lakes
Filling fields and country roads in an unwanted baptism

Hear the night wind blow
Nothing can stop it
Nothing can halt its progress
Nothing can thwart its tempestuous advance

Onward it goes
Gusting furiously towards a neon lit city
Sixty miles inland

Do not trifle with its ways
Do not resist its relentless course
Do not fight this ferocious beast of the air
Lest you be tossed aside like a broken rag doll

Hear the chill wind blow
As it sweeps onward toward a midnight horizon
Leaving colossal airborne destruction in its wake[61]

---

[61] This poem was written on Monday 27th September 2010

NIGHTFALL AT SCARBOROUGH

The sun dips beneath a slightly choppy sea
Casting a last broad shaft of shimmering, sensual scarlet
Into a quickly darkening sky

Gently rolling waves leave ragged lines of foam
Whilst the swishing, swashing, soaking sea
Turns from grey blue into inky black

Bright distant stars shine into view
As wispy high clouds
Reflect a last ray of pink

Garish multi-coloured seaside lights
Curve like a gaudy necklace
Around a sandy, seaweed-strewn bay

They merge with the orange neon baubles
Of a noisy harbour-side fairground;
Man's earthbound light huddled beneath starlight

The muffled whirr of a Ferris wheel,
Barely heard because of the metallic clatter of slot machines
And the distant screams of a pleasure-loving people

A discarded newspaper rustles on a cliff top seat
And is suddenly whisked, topsy-turvy along
By a light, warm breeze

Encircling seagulls chirrup, squawk and cry
Scavengers of the now blackening sky
Greedy for food provided by man and nature

From far away wafts the mouth watering aroma
Of fresh fish and chips
A most traditional Scarborough fare

Small groups of people saunter aimlessly
In loose fitting jackets
Or fluttering woollen cardigans

A tired, angry mother slaps a sullen-faced child
Whose wail of self-pity
Noisily pierces the air

Another child's protest is blocked by a long stick of rock
Which juts out of his mouth
Like a concrete cigar

Time was when our children were that age
Now they're hulking teenagers
Too embarrassed to be seen with *'mum'* and *'dad'*

Sand-worn buckets and spades lie neglected
At the bottom of a cupboard,
The time for family holidays is now past

Old memories crowd in of hilarious beach games
And fun swims in the sea watched by a (now departed) Grandfather
Only the endless requests for money remain the same

It's nightfall at Scarborough,
A place my wife and I will not revisit
For an unknown span of years –
A place crowded by memories
Of a very happy past[62]

---

[62] This piece was written in Beverley, Yorkshire on Sunday, 24th August 2003, the day after our final family holiday at Scarborough – a resort we had visited every August since 1987. It explores the sorrow felt when leaving a well loved place for the last time.

NIGHTMARE SHOPPING

Eye's flick anxiously
From side to side
A snub nose
Twitches up and down
Her face assumes a
'Goofy bunny rabbit look'

Colour starts to drain from her cheeks
Worry lines criss-cross a furrowed forehead
Lips lock into an anxious martyr's frown
As she fearfully creeps into the yawning mouth
Of a clothes shop

A frightening fate has to be faced
A terrible trial must be endured
A life or death decision has to be made
In which seconds freeze into long, paralysing hours

For;

In this clothes shop
She will have to choose
Yes choose!
Whether to select
That white dress
Or that cream dress
(Of the same design)
For a wedding
She has to attend[63]

---

[63] This poem was written on Thursday, 23rd April 2009 following an exasperating shopping expedition with my wife.

NO, MY DEAR

No, my dear
You're not fat,
Just pleasantly round

No, my dear
You're not frumpy,
Just slightly dowdy

No, my dear
You're not haggard,
Just a trifle *'shop worn'*

No, my dear
Your hair isn't a mess,
Just looks like a bird's nest

No, my dear
Your meal isn't too cold,
Just a trifle tepid

No, my dear
You're not getting old,
Just ageing somewhat

No, my dear
You don't get on my nerves
Just aggravate them

No, my dear
You're not a useless wife,
Just a bit incapable

But why do YOU say *"No!"* my dear,
Have I said something to offend you?[64]

---

[64] This piece was written on Friday, May 30th 2003 and looks at the theme of male insensitivity.

NORTHERN SCOTLAND

Northern Scotland!

A land of
Cruel blizzards
Wet clammy mists
Gorgeous warm sunshine and
Torrential downpours

Northern Scotland!

A land of
Rugged coastlines
Small fishing ports
Noisy white seagulls and
Spectacular cliffs

Northern Scotland!

A land of
Rolling hills
Lush green glens
Forbidding grey mountains and
Purple heather

Northern Scotland!

A land of
Boggy marshes
Black water lochs
Well hidden wildlife and
Forest plantations

Northern Scotland!

A land of
Abandoned castles
Shaggy brown cattle
Futile clan revolts and
Clannish feuds

Northern Scotland!

A land of
Green conservation
Dying Calvinist values
Post Modern pretensions and
Capitalist enterprise

Northern Scotland!

A land of
Embalmed tradition
Bleeping mobile phones
Purring mountain railways and
Costly restaurants

Northern Scotland!

A land of
Squat Churches
Grey stone houses
Hydro-Electric dams and
Luxury Hotels

Northern Scotland!

A land of
Succulent haggis
Mouth burning whisky
Asian takeaway food and
Tesco's supermarkets

Northern Scotland!

A land of
Warm hospitality
Costly tourist traps
'Och-noo' accents and
Plaited kilts

Northern Scotland!

A land of
International tourism
English holiday campers
Small town globalisation and
Foreign skiers

Northern Scotland!

A land of
Long queues
Crowded Visitor Centres
Noisy coach parties and
Ringing tills

Northern Scotland!

A land where locals
Take money from outsiders
In the nicest possible way![65]

---

[65] This meditation was written on Tuesday, 24th August 2004, at Pitlochry Scotland. Its theme is the different characteristics of Northern Scotland.

OH, MR BLAIR

Oh, Mr Blair
There's so much hot air
It's too much to bear

You did so much care
About your dare
Things aren't fair
Under the bright media glare
No wonder you're losing your hair –

The foe is still in his lair
It's become a nightmare

Your situation has gone the shape of a pear
Even with your wife you feel you can't share
She has that queasy wild-eyed stare
Whilst this nation you tear

Oh, Mr Blair, you wonder where
But there's no hope anywhere
So Mr Blair, DO beware.[66]

---

[66] This poem was written on Friday, March 7th 2003 during the run-up to the Anglo-American invasion of Iraq. The then British Prime Minister, Tony Blair was enduring a great deal of personal political pressure surrounding the invasion of Iraq.

OLD BROWN BOOK

You look very sexy lying in bed
Reading that old brown book on medical dissections
With its tatty hardback cover

I love you to bits
I love you to bits

Looking so inviting yet
Paying rapt attention to that thick brown book on medical
dissections
With its musty, yellowed pages

I love you to bits
I love you to bits

What can I do but adore and love you
As you studiously ignore me in favour of that worn brown book on
medical dissections
With its old sketches of human body parts

I love you to bits
I love you to bits

I just want to caress and touch you
Instead you say *"please make me a cup of nice hot tea"*
A quick smile
Then it's back to that old, thick, worn brown book on medical
dissections
You in your world, me in mine[67]

---

[67] This meditation was written on Sunday, 30th October 2007. It expresses the longing felt by the writer for his wife as she was preoccupied reading one of her Medical History Books.

ORDER OF CONVERSATION

1.

What do young ladies talk about in their spare time?

Relationships, families and ailments – in that order

What do mature ladies talk about in their spare time?

Families, relationships and ailments – in that order

What do old ladies talk about in their spare time?

Ailments, families and relationships – in that order

Together, these topics make up 90% of female conversation – men respond by burying their heads in the newspaper or by watching sport on TV[68]

2.

What do young men talk about in their spare time?

Sex, sport and politics – in that order

What do mature men talk about in their spare time?

Sport, sex and politics – in that order

What do old men talk about in their spare time?

Politics, sport and their bladders – in that order

Together, these topics make up 90% of male conversation – women respond by burying themselves in the kitchen or by chatting to friends on the phone[69]

---

[68] This poem was written on Tuesday, 23rd February 2010. It was provoked by having my 86 year old mother and a 91 year old lady for Sunday lunch on 14th February 2010. They had begun vying with each other as to who had the most ailments.
[69] This second part was written on Monday 10th May 2010 following my wife's suggestion that I should *'do a similar one for men.'*

PERPLEXITY

Deep are the emotions of a woman
Unfathomable are its motives
Unpredictable are its ways
Unsatisfied are its yearnings

How can they be examined
How can they be probed
How can they be satisfied –
Even by the greatest act of love?[70]

---

[70] This meditation was written on Monday, 28th August 2006 whilst staying at Berwick-Upon-Tweed and expresses the perplexity many husbands feel when confronted by the emotional needs of their wives.

POST MODERN BLUES

Bonjour y name eez Professor Bidet Bordello
(No relation to Michael Portillo)
I'm ze profound, philosophical post moderneest
Wiz words I love to geeve a leetle tweest

My books are all in fashion now
— But don't ask me how —
Baudillard, Foucault and Saussure were my teachers
They are post capitalist, post modern, post everyzing preachers
Linguistic analysis is what I engage in
Stripping words of zere meaning is completely my theeng

Let's dive into hyper-reeality
Which we will explore with great feedelity
Employing the methods of semantic deconstruction
(Adjective meaning *I'll bring to destruction*)
Boldly we'll leap into existential unreason
(To a moderneest that is intellectual treason)
My only narratee is that there is no meta-narrateeve
Paradoxically, it's a meta-narrateeve that denies all meta-narrateeves
That will be my discourse, of course
Which I shall explain weez some force

So let's be bold
And place ze subjective concept of common sense on hold
All life is an ironic feection
It's many symbols engage in dialectic freection
Thesis must give birth to anti-thesis
Which then must give birth to synthesis
Which becomes another thesis
History must come to an end
But don't let that drive you round ze bend
Already we live in post history
I trust that's not too much of a mystery
Such concepts as 'history' are the subjective invention of Man
Man is the invention of Man,
Patriarchy is the invention of Man
Reality is the invention of Man

The notion of truth is the invention of Man
It has no existence outside of ze mind of Man
But the word *'Man'*
Is something feminists would like to *'ban'*
As a concept it's problematical
Linguistically, it's hardly grammatical

Take zee menu here
Ze prices aren't very dear
It's caption is an example of Po-Mo art
It doesn't really look all that smart
But we can still explore its semiology
Whilst looking at its underlying epistemology
It's symboleec system is paradigmaticaly related
Old prices can be easily deleted
Notice its syntagmatic combination
(No! thees lecture is not an abomination!)
The leest of foodstuffs are signifiers
To be precise, metanonic signifiers
Signified is the signifier's significators
Which is a very significant signifier
Adding value to the meal
Whilst symboliseeng a very good deal
There's no obvious metaphor
But customers are enticed to want more
Thees seemple menu
Belongs to a specifeec cultural venue
As ze great Michael Foucault said –
Before he was died
From visits to Nath Houses: -
"The criteria of Epistemes
Can be defined through what or whom they disqualify
In the case of Modernity –
The mad, the sick
And the criminal."
Admittedly, Foucault was sadeestic
In his meta-episteemeec
But he showed how all values were a social construczeon
Capable of bringing great destruczeon
So let's celebrate diversity

No matter what the perversity
Multi-culturaleesm is the way to go
So let's geeve it one last throw
Absolute right or wrong do not exeest

It's absolutely wrong to allow such myths to persist
In our thinking let's turn to the East
On Monistic Pantheism let us feast
Let's move into zee universal simulacrum
Taking that as our rule of thumb

So what is *'Post Modernism?'* you ask
You really do set me a difficult task
Oh very well,
But giving a clear definition is hell,
Put very simply Post Moderneesm is the meaningless explanazeon
Of that meaninglessness
Which is the offshoot of Modernistic Meaninglessness
Reflecteeng the cosmic meaninglessness of life

There, ze meaning should be very clear
Oh, don't complain that it's all too queer
For the knowledge I geeve you is very deep
You have no excuse to fall asleep
Post Modernism is ze way ahead
And a lot could still be said
But now I must take ze *'final bow'*
For...
Zere there are other audiences I need to *'wow'*
I thank you all for your rapt attention
Au revoir mez amies[71]

---

[71] This poem was written on Saturday, 13th September 2008 and is best read in a pretentious French accent.

PROOF READING WIFE

There you sit *'bunched up'*
In the corner of our guest house bedroom
Red biro clasped tightly in your fingers
Attentive look from gravy brown eyes
Headaches temporarily forgotten

You are the loveliest of women
The most devoted of wives

Your red biro darts across the paper
Amending a word here
Correcting a word there
Massacring muddled sentences
Slaughtering unwanted phrases

You are the loveliest of women
The most devoted of wives

With furrowed head you pause, before pruning out
An ambiguous word, which has revolted
A technical term, which has rebelled
A new concept, which has retaliated

You are the loveliest of women
The most devoted of wives

A sigh! A *'tut!'*
A look of exasperation in your eyes
Is it really that bad?
Scribbling resumes, a headache is held back whilst
A helpful suggestion is thrown into the line space
An impatient remark is written in the margin
A sarcastic comment is placed beside a sentence
The semantic insurgency has been quelled

You are the loveliest of women
The most devoted of wives
A proof-reader beyond compare…
Now will you please correct this silly poem?[72]

---

[72] This poem was written the day before our twenty-sixth wedding anniversary on Wednesday, 22nd June 2005 in the bedroom of a Guest House in Beverley, East Yorkshire. Its theme is the need to appreciate a good proof-reading wife.

REINSTATEMENT

I'm back! I'm back!
I'm jolly well back

I'm back! I'm back!
Prepared for the attack

I'm back! I'm back!
Get ready for some flack

I'm back! I'm back!
No time to grab my Mac

I'm back! I'm back!
Hurry! Got important papers to pack

I'm back! I'm back!
No longer on the rack

I'm back! I'm back!
No need to fear the sack

I'm back! I'm back!
I punch the air with a jolly smack

I'm back! I'm back!
Now on the right track

I'm back! I'm back!
Won't have to do my 'whack'

I'm back! I'm back!
I'm certainly taken aback

Now it's you who'll face the sack[73]

---

[73] This poem was written on Friday, May 23rd 2003, after first coming to mind during a long swim on my back at a large International Swimming Pool. It's about an influential person being cleared by an Official Enquiry. He has been restored to a high position, now free from any worries of being sent to prison.

REPRISE: AT FORTY-SEVEN

At forty-seven I found myself a Poet
Words exploding from my heart
Youthful talent now revived
Wonderland vistas opening up
For at forty-seven, I've begun[74]

RESISTING THE WATERS

Running waters
Resisting rocks
Endless erosion
Deepening gully
Landscape changes

Nature in flux
The waters triumph
Over the rocks
As they seek
A distant sea[75]

---

[74] This reprise was written in my bedroom on the morning of Friday, June 5th 2003.
[75] This poem was written on Ilkely Moor on Bank Holiday Monday, 25th May 2009. I'd been sitting on some rocks overlooking the Addingham aspect of the Wharfedale valley.

RUINED MIND

Drawn and fearful mother at the bedside
Her son's head smashed through a windscreen
Brain splattered like clotted cream
Zombie state now his fate

Ruined mind, blighted life

Father, out for a smoke
Busy nurses bustle by
Stricken mother wants to cry
She can take no more of this mental gore

Ruined mind, blighted life

Age Twenty-Two, all hope of future gone
Prison-four corners of a bed
Doctors have left much unsaid
Blue uniformed sister hurries along
Engaged intently on her round

Ruined mind, blighted life

Mystery of suffering now portrayed
Kindly chaplain offers a prayer
Tries to ease this bedside nightmare
Two eternal years now gone by inert son breathes a faint sigh

Ruined mind, blighted life

Higher cortex centres long destroyed
Spittle from his mouth – watch it slowly run
He used to be quite a lad, so full of fun
May death soon come for their brain-damaged, only son!

Ruined mind, blighted life[76]

---

[76] This poem was written on Friday, October 26th 1990, and was inspired by a conversation with a mother whom I met wheeling her son through a hospital corridor. Most details were reconstructed from my own imagination. It expresses the despair and hopelessness caused by long-term suffering.

SEVEN AGES OF MAN

In your teens you try to learn all
In your twenties you think you know all
In your thirties you hope you know all
In your forties you know you don't know all
In your fifties you begin to understand all
In your sixties you <u>do</u> understand all
But;
In your seventies you either acquire wisdom or
You begin to lose it all[77]

SEVEN WOMEN

There are seven types of women I could never marry
The selfish woman who loves pleasure
The shouting woman who nags and scolds
The smoking woman who just has to have her fags
The sorrowful woman who moans about her ailments
The sour woman who loves to harbour a grievance
The stupid woman who keeps an untidy house
The superstitious woman who believes in horoscopes

All seven I would gladly push under a bus!

There are seven types of women I would love to marry
The calm woman who doesn't get on my nerves
The capable woman who gets things done
The clever woman who stimulates good ideas
The cooking woman who prepares a lovely meal (yum-yum!)
The companionable woman who talks and amuses
The compassionate woman who is busy doing good
The conscientious woman who looks after me

All seven I met in my lovely wife![78]

---

[77] This poem was written on Friday, 22nd January 2010.
[78] This piece was written on Tuesday, 10th February 2004 and warns against courting an unsuitable woman. It also expresses the sense of thankfulness generated by a happy marriage.

SHORELINE DEBRIS

Debris from the land
Debris from the sea
Debris from the city
Debris from the country
There's debris everywhere on the Humber Estuary

Debris on the beach
Debris on the mudflats
Debris dropped by ships
Debris dropped by visitors
There's debris everywhere on the Humber Estuary

Debris buried beneath the sand
Debris exposed to view
Debris from the war
Debris from times of peace
There's debris everywhere on the Humber Estuary

Debris from the past
Debris from the present
Debris that will decay
Debris that will last
There's debris everywhere on the Humber Estuary[79]

---

[79] This poem was written on Monday 28th June 2010 after walking around Spurn Head Peninsula and noticing the debris on the beach, including a yellow *'sou wester'* that had evidently been dropped from a ship.

SPIN DOCTOR

I am the *'Doctor of Spin'*
Who obeys his master's every whim
The general public I scorn as dim
A web of half-truths I eagerly manufacture
A cluster-bomb of lies I scatter
Misleading assurances are my forte
Sly innuendoes my expertise
I know how to damn with faint praise
I know what *'bad news to bury'*
I know which successes to broadcast
I know what good *'sound bites'* to give
As an informed source
(Privy to inside information)
There is much news to fabricate
All for a healthy cause!
The shadows are where I dwell
Backroom intrigues are my love
Ceaseless plotting my game
With a *'non-attributable'* comment
I can destroy my master's enemies
(Or my Own)
Oh, I adore the thrill of power
The influential ear to bend
The story to invent
The reputation to subtly undermine;
I know when to threaten
Whom to cajole
How to flatter
I know when to tell the risqué joke
To be *'one of the lads;'*
Infinitely adaptable am I
Putty in my master's hands
Flexibility is my strength
A knighthood or peerage in view
A demeanour of modesty I must assume –
Bowing and scraping
Crawling and fawning
Calling her dear Majesty *'Maam!'*

Dark secrets are safe with me –
For payment of a large fee
Your firm friend I will be
There is no such thing as *'truth'*
Only media representation
Aided by slick presentation
My only god is *'self'*
A Post Modernist am I
No matter what that may signify
As a Philosophy it's most convenient
Its view of things I find expedient.
My master of course I will betray
When he starts to wobble
From high office I will help him topple.
A new master will find my services indispensable
(Watch out if he doesn't!)
Frank memoirs I will publish
On the poor Spin Doctor's plight
These will tell all and
Yet say nothing.
Into the limelight I will tread
With a bold strutting step
My soul I will bare
Through a lot of hot air
Royalty cheques to gain
A taste of five-minute fame;
Under the bright studio light
I will look a well-groomed sight
A confessional interview to make
Whilst always busy *'on the take'*
My own praises I will sing
For I am the Doctor of Spin –
Do obey my every whim![80]

---

[80] This poem was written on Wednesday, June 4th 2003, whilst travelling by bus from Central Manchester to Didsbury. Its theme is the amorality existing in much of modern politics.

TARGET

First, came the exclusion – the target was isolated

Second, came the persecution – the target was harmed

Third, came the extermination – the target was killed

Mass murder is easy to arrange – once you know how[81]

---

[81] This meditation was written on Tuesday, 31st May 2005. It explores how genocide occurs in neat incremental steps. The concluding line was added on Wednesday, 7th April 2010.

TEENAGE TORY DREAMS

Limp hair parted
Old-fashioned glasses
Thin youthful build

Hands clasped behind head
Lying on top of his neatly made bed
Gazing fondly at his latest pin up

Eagerly he dreams
An uncommon fantasy
Of true love

Hands clasped behind head
Lying on top of his neatly made bed
Gazing fondly at his latest pin up

Home Counties birth
Successful millionaire parents
Private School education,

Hands clasped behind head
Lying on top of his neatly made bed
Gazing fondly at his latest pin up

Excellent school marks
Oxbridge his goal
Law he'll sit

Hands clasped behind head
Lying on top of his neatly made bed
Gazing fondly at his latest pin up

City career ahead
Influence to gain
Reputation to make

Hands clasped behind head
Lying on top of his neatly made bed
Gazing fondly at his latest pin up

Will work very hard
Be elected for Parliament
Nice safe seat,

Hands clasped behind head
Lying on top of his neatly made bed
Gazing fondly at his latest pin up

Chief Whips favour?
Hard won promotion?
Cabinet post maybe?

Hands clasped behind head
Lying on top of his neatly made bed
Gazing fondly at his latest pin up
Of ex Prime Minister, Margaret Thatcher[82]

---

[82] This poem was written on Saturday, June 7th 2003, whilst travelling by bus from Central Manchester to Didsbury. Its theme is the hold political ambitions can have on people, even at a young age.

THE ABSENT MUSE

~~Beside the merry bubbling brook~~
~~I sit~~
~~Listening to its melodic waters~~
~~Sweetly play~~

"No, no, no that's not good enough – cross it out and try again!"

~~In yonder valley cutting~~
~~I crouch~~
~~Contemplating mother nature's bounteous beauty~~

"Rubbish! Let's try a third time – this time I'll close my eyes and listen to the water."

~~Ah, how merrily~~
~~Does the blessed, bubbling brook run~~
~~Its playful waters licking against...~~

'LICK! LICK! LICK!'

'What's this black Labrador doing licking my cheek! Now – be off with you!'

'WOOF! WOOF! WOOF!'

"Go back to your owner and don't flick that wet tail of yours in my face!"

~~Hear the innocent children play~~
~~Merrily splashing in the stream~~

'SPLASH'

"Did I splash you Mister?"
(Quizzes a little boy
With the black inscribed words 'Explosive Talent!'
Inscribed on his yellow T-shirt)

"Yes you did!"

"What are you doing Mister – writing on that bit of paper?"

"Writing a poem about nature and NICE, well behaved children."

"We write poems at school Mister! Teacher says they're right good, she gives me a gold star – are yours any good Mister?"

"If I'm given the time to write them!"

"Teacher gives us a prize if we write a real good 'un. Do you get a prize?"

Only the Hughes and Larkin happy poet prize!"

"Who are they Mister?"

"You'll find out soon enough. Now go back to your daddy!"

"But I haven't got a daddy."

"Then go back to your mother, or whoever's looking after you!"

~~Oh hear the soft dulcet tones~~
~~Of Mother as she calls for her child~~
~~Full of dear sweet grace and maternal love she cries...~~

"Where do you think you've been, yer little bleeder – I've told yer many a time not to wander off!"

"But Mam!"

"SLAP!"

'WAIL!!!'

~~Watch the sheep contentedly chew hillside grass~~
~~As lambs gambol playfully behind them~~
~~Bleating gently...~~

'BAAH! BAAH! BAAH!'

"*Does that sheep above me have to bleat so loudly – it's not as if I'm going to have it for a lamb chop?*"

'*BAAH! BAAH! BAAH!*'

'*BAAH! BAAH! BLINKING BAAH! Now go away otherwise I'll chuck this pebble – there!*'

'*BAAH! Baah! Baah!*'

'*That's got rid of it! Now back to my poem!*"

~~Hear the silence of the countryside~~
~~Become part of the peace it brings~~
~~Escape the noisy vicissitudes of city life~~
~~Hush now and enjoy the quiet~~

'*ROAR!*'

'*I would have to try and write a poem*
Under the flight path from Yeadon airport!"

~~See a hawk-like bird~~
~~Glide in the heavens above~~
~~Watch it begin to swoop upon its prey~~
~~Suddenly, it drops...~~

'*PLOP!*'

"*Did it have to drop its 'poo' on my paper?*"

~~Majestic, mountainous clouds~~
~~Tower above~~
~~Offering to slake the thirst~~
~~Of a parched, powdery earth~~
~~A gentle pitter-patter of rain~~
~~Falls to refresh Mother Nature's thirsty ground~~

"*Oh no! A sudden downpour! A gentle pitter-patter I said – not this soaking deluge! I'll have to stop if it continues like this!*"

~~"Boom! Boom! Boom! Boom! Boom! Boom!~~
~~Hear the far off thunder peel~~

'BOOOOM!!!CRASH!!!'

"Wow! that was dangerously close – almost above my head!"

~~Admire the gorgeous pink lightening strike~~
~~As it flashers across a sombre brooding sky~~

'FLASH! BOOM!!!'

'That's it! It's time to leave – I'm off! I don't want any more of my poem turning into reality.'

'FLAAASH! BOOOOM!'

~~End of poem~~

End of poet?[83]

---

[83] This poem was written on Ilkely Moor beside a fast flowing stream on Bank Holiday Monday, 25th May 2009. Some of the incidents described in it are deliberately exaggerated though based upon real-life encounters I had experienced that day.

THE ANCESTRAL MILL

I stand alone in the old village Corn Mill
Dead wheat husks spilling from my warm open hand
Old, rusting machinery brooding in the corner
Relics of a long-forgotten, industrial age
Where real men did real work
Rodent life scratches and scampers into hidden holes,
A noisy crow calls out from its nest in the broken roof
'Kraaar! Kraaar! Kraaar!'
Warm shafts of sunlight pierce through
Small grubby window panes
And off-white paint peels and flakes
From crumbling sandstone walls
Only the spiders are busy
Weaving their silver webs
Like busy mill girls
Intent on their looms

Cautiously

I clamber up a rickety worm-eaten ladder
To examine the roof area
From where sacks of grain were once dropped
Now rotting and splintered floorboards
Creak and sag beneath my weight
No machines here
Only dust, grey sacking and
The droppings of a family of crows
Whose mother still cries forlornly
'Kraaar! Kraaar! Kraaar!'

Suddenly,

Through the haze of choking dust
Noise, hustle and bustle return
Flour covered men in old country attire
Humping and heaving sacks of grain,
Exchanging winks and glances
One cuffs a small boy on his snowy white ear

120

A horse neighs and snorts from below and
The clatter of machinery thunders upwards
The strained creak of a pulley,
Heavily weighed down with sack loads of grain
Lifted from the cart below
Busy industrial England brought back to life again

Then

Emptiness returns
Once more I am alone
Except for the crow who still cries forlornly
'Kraaar! Kraaar! Kraaar!'
A man of the twenty first century
Quietly surveying the mill where
His ancestors had toiled[84]

---

[84] This meditation, written on Friday, 24th December 2004 was based upon a visit the writer had made to a derelict West Yorkshire Corn Mill once worked in by his ancestors on Saturday, July 26th 2003. It was revised in response to criticism on Thursday, 13th January 2005. It examines how historical research can stir the imagination.

THE EMPTY BEDROOM

An empty bedroom
An empty bed
And empty drawers
Which had once bulged with his clothes

An empty computer table
An empty compact disc rack
And empty walls
With only splodges of *'blue tack'*
To show where his posters had been

An empty book shelf
An empty waste bin
And empty parental hearts
Feeling a mixture of desolation and relief
Now that his mess had
At last, been cleared

Only the wall cupboard
Still bulged with his things
Awaiting removal to his new town centre apartment
All crammed together
In tightly packed array;
Science Fiction videos
Fantasy computer games
Coiled-up pieces of wire
Scuffed exercise books
And battered school text books
Covering every period of education
From early secondary
To second year university

Layers of his life
Represented in that bulging cupboard
One day, it too will be empty[85]

---

[85] This poem was written on Sunday, 21st September 2008, the day after my wife and I had spent almost fourteen hours clearing out our youngest son's bedroom after he'd left home at the age of twenty.

THE GATHERING

One burst tyre
One quick skid
One deadly mistake

A party of rescue workers
Blue lights flashing
Sirens whirring
Hurrying to yet another accident scene
On the Manchester bound lane of
The M62 Motorway

Three crashed cars
Four dead bodies
(One unidentifiable)

A party of rescue workers
Gathered on a stormy, sleet-snowing night
On the Manchester bound lane of
The M62 Motorway

Three ambulances
Two Fire Engines
One Police Car

Gathered around
A crash site of death
Where petrol fumes hover
On the Manchester bound lane of
The M62 Motorway

Three bereaved families
Three different funerals
Three injured children
(One permanently crippled)

Parties of black clad mourners
Gather to grieve for
The loved ones they lost
During that ice-cloaked night
On the Manchester bound lane of
The M62 Motorway[86]

---

[86] This poem was written as a sequel to *Black Snake Motorway* during a snowy evening on Saturday, 7th February 2004 whilst travelling by coach from Manchester (to Leeds) the writer had passed a horrendous crash site on the M62 Motorway.

THE JOLLY HOBGOBLIN

There was once a country pub
'The Jolly Hobgoblin' by name
Complete with a painted sign
Depicting the face of a cheerful woman in glasses
With a knowing, mischievous smile

This lady was Anthea
Who'd once served as
A much liked barmaid
Full of 'Dears' and 'Dah-lings'
As she'd pulled pints of Traditional Ale
With a rather strong hand,
Listening with feigned patience to elderly men
Moaning about their wives who didn't understand them

When rushing to meet an order
She would shout
'I'm coming as fast as my little legs will let me!'

Rumour had it that she'd once been a gossip columnist
On a local newspaper
She'd even got involved in some big news story
About an Anthrax scare –
A suspicious parcel having arrived on her desk...
Fortunately containing only a couple of Andrex toilet rolls

In her time in the media
She'd known anybody who was anybody
And was always willing to tell a good yarn
About the tricks she'd played as a journalist
Getting half naked men and their sons
To appear at their front doors
So that photographs could be taken of them
Her tales had often provided 'comic relief'
To otherwise dispirited pub customers

One night a ferocious gale
Had blown the previous sign down
(Which had been of a pair of muddy hiking boots
From the days when the pub
Had been called *The Jolly Walker*)
And one of the regulars
A middle aged bachelor
(Who happened to be a sign writer by trade)
Had painted the new one
Saying that it would cheer everyone up

He became the new Landlord
With Anthea once again pulling the Ale
Listening with feigned patience to mature ladies
Moaning about their husbands who didn't understand them

Rumour has it that she's just begun
A new web site entitled
'Auntie Anthea's Agony Advice Bureau'
And when asked about it
All she does is quietly catch your eye, smile and say
'It's none of your business, dah-ling!'[87]

---

[87] This poem was written on Sunday, 22nd June 2008 whilst staying with my wife at a Guesthouse in Halifax. She'd asked me to compose a light-hearted poem about her friend – hence the underlying sense of humour.

THE LOCAL FOX

The local fox pricks up his ears,
Birds squawk, loud and clamorous,
Startled by a prowling black cat
With twitching whiskers and a wild fixed stare
Muffled canine barks are heard from inside
From inside a local red bricked house
Whose unkempt garden
Slopes gently downward
Toward a deep rail cutting
Where feral youths with shaven heads
Love to lurk
Drinking cider, lager and beer
To escape the boring futility
Of their existence

Then, a sharp whistle
The rails whisper
Their metallic warning

Suddenly a steam train
Thunders from an echoing tunnel archway
Billowing, chuffing, clattering, steaming noisily past
An empty suburban station
Mini-tornados
Swirling around the platform
Fling pockets of litter up into the air

On and on it travels
Into a far horizon
Made crimson by a blood-red sunset
Leaving behind a dissolving cloud of soot-smelling steam

Its whistle
Also no more than a fading echo
Rebounding on the unkempt
Debris-strewn embankment
Where the local fox still has his lair[88]

---

[88] This meditation was written on Wednesday, 9th January 2008. It expresses the mixture of rural and urban life hidden just out of sight in any city suburb.

THE NORMAL POET

Ah-hem!
Please do excuse me
I er apologise for
This most awkward presentation
But you see I have
A rather embarrassing problem
I am afraid to admit it
But I'm sadly a normal poet!
I dress like an accountant,
I look like an accountant
Even worse, I like it that way
At night
My strongest drink is a cup of cocoa
Nicely flavoured with sugar
My only vice is a fondness for train spotting
No hint of scandal spoils my life
(Mother sees to that!)
Afraid to say the tabloids would find me most dull
The only drugs I take
Are aspirins for my headaches

In the world of poetry
I try to be ever so nice
I criticise no one
Nor engage in poetry politics
(Whatever they are)
On such matters I am, 'ahem' rather innocent
Naïve you may think

During my recitals
Expect no flowing beard,
No wild-eyed stare or booming voice
No funny props or
Me dressed only in my underpants
Have no hope that
I will electrify an audience with my charisma
I haven't got any
My verses are strictly of the soothing kind

My normality vexes other poets
I'm sorry to be so anti-bohemian
But being dull is my pleasure
Besides why should freakishness
Ever be mistaken for talent?

'Get a life' you may reply
But, you see, I already have one
Happily living with mother and
Tiddles the cat![89]

---

[89] This meditation was written on Wednesday, 28th September 2005. The original inspiration came from seeing old footage of some *'Beat'* poets in Martin Scorsee's documentary on the songwriter Bob Dylan. (Broadcast on BBC2, Monday, 26th and Tuesday, 27th September 2005). It portrays the pretentiousness displayed by some of these poets.

THE OLD, OLD CAT

I am the old, old cat
Whose once sleek black fur
Is now bedraggled brown tat,
My elderly mistress can't hear me purr.

On a sun-drenched window sill,
I carelessly flop
Lying ever so still
So afraid I might drop

My joints ache with rheumatic pain,
Mice I no longer want to catch
As every shape looks the same.
A nap is all I want to snatch

I long to sleep and not wake-up
My bladder I no longer control
It all makes me feel so fed-up
To even bother with a stroll

Look and see
Because...
One day, you'll be like me[90]

---

[90] This poem first arose after seeing an elderly cat lying fast asleep on a window sill at Shaldon, near Teignmouth, South Devon on Tuesday, 18th August 2009.

THE UNWANTED CALLER

Pull down the blinds!
Draw the curtains!
Switch off the lights
Turn on the alarm!
Hide the women!
Unchain the guard dogs!
Don't answer the bell!
Pretend you're not in!
Hide your wallet!

For an MP is calling round
To canvass for your votes...[91]
Is that all he really wants?[92]

THINGS

There are things to face
There are things to avoid
We must know the difference[93]

---

[91] Readers are welcome to alter this and the previous line should they wish to refer to some other public nuisance or *'hate figure.'*
[92] This poem was written on Bank Holiday Monday, 25th May 2009 on a wooden table outside *'The White Cafe'* following some long walks on Ilkely Moor. A public scandal over MP expenses claims had been raging at the time.
[93] This observation was written on Saturday, 11th October 2008.

THIRTEEN SIGNS

When you see...

Bigotry
Mistaken
For
Virtue

Cowardice
Mistaken
For
Wisdom

Delusion
Mistaken
For
Hope

Display
Mistaken
For
Wealth

Enslavement
Mistaken
For
Liberation

Fanaticism
Mistaken
For
Faith

Fantasy
Mistaken
For
Reality

Lust
Mistaken
For
Love

Novelty
Mistaken
For
Invention

Obscenity
Mistaken
For
Humour

Pornography
Mistaken
For
Culture

Rudeness
Mistaken
For
Honesty

Violence
Mistaken
For
Assertion

You will
Have seen
Thirteen signs
Of decadence[94]

---

[94] This meditation was written in late October 1975 and rediscovered (on Tuesday, 5th October 2004) in an old file scrawled on some undergraduate philosophy notes. It was substantially re-worked on Monday, 18th October 2004 and highlights the need to know the symptoms of a decadent society.

THREE WISHES

I wish I could make you happy
I wish I could calm your nerves
I wish I could settle your anxiety
But things just seem to stay the same

Instead, all I can do
My sloppy *'ha'porth,'*
Is just to give you
A kiss and a cuddle
Whilst saying *'I love you'*
Mmmm![95]

---

[95] This meditation was written on Sunday, 2nd March 2008 when the writer's wife was suffering from one of her headaches.

TO MY FATHER

You were the best of fathers
Wise, gentle and compassionate
A gentleman
A *'toff'*
A *'distinguished looking fellow'*
Always neatly attired in a dark three piece suit or
Checked sports jacket
The foundation of all that I am
The imparter of excellent moral values
The man of many wise judgements
Who, by example
Showed me the
Right way to go
Whilst giving me a hatred of falsehood or
What you would call, *'bull'*

My only regret now
Is that I can't openly share with you
My successes, nor let you know
How I inwardly feel your influence even more today
Than when you were alive
But from the standpoint of eternity
You perhaps already know
And are delighted to see the good things
Your life on earth has produced[96]

---

[96] This poem was written on Tuesday, 20th April 2004, soon after the fifth anniversary commemorating the death of my father. It expresses my heartfelt desire to share my personal successes with him.

TOO BUSY

First they aborted the unborn
But I was too busy having a good time to care

Then they starved those in a vegetative state
But I was too busy having a good time to care

Then they denied asylum seekers their right to work
But I was too busy having a good time to care

Then they imposed new techniques of surveillance
But I was too busy having a good time to care

Then they sanctioned the torture of suspects
But I was too busy having a good time to care

Then they restricted freedom of speech
But I was too busy having a good time to care

Then they picked on vulnerable minorities
But I was too busy having a good time to care

Then they imposed internal passports
But I was too busy having a good time to care

Then they took people all around me
But I was too busy having a good time to care

Then they came for me
But everyone else was too busy having a good time to care[97]

---

[97] This poem was written on Wednesday, October 8th 2008. It represents a modified and updated version of Pastor Martin Niemoller's poem *'First they came for the Jews.'*

TRASHED

Bad!
Mad!
Sad!

Bashed!
Smashed!
Trashed!

Battered!
Shattered!
Tattered!

Drained!
Pained!
Shamed!

Is how I feel
About not getting that job
I hoped for

Is my despair really beyond repair?[98]

---

[98] This meditation was written on Thursday, 7th October 2004, two days after a much sought after job had fallen through. It expresses the dismay felt in the aftermath of a failed job application.

TWEEDLECAM AND TWEEDLECLEGG

Tweedlecam and Tweedleclegg
fought a very naughty electoral battle!
For Tweedlecam said to Tweedleclegg
'You stole Mr Blair's nice spinning rattle!'
'Oh no I didn't!' replied Tweedleclegg
'Oh yes you did!' said Tweedlecam

Just then a dark Scottish crow flew down
As black as a tar-barrel!
He frightened both our heroes into an anxious frown,
so they quite forgot their quarrel.

Now Tweedlecam and Tweedleclegg
Are the very best of friends[99]

---

[99] This adaption of a poem (found in chapter four of Lewis Carroll's *Through the Looking Glass*) was written on Tuesday, 3rd August 2010. It was provoked by watching a BBC documentary concerning the formation of the Conservative and Liberal Coalition Government which had emerged five days after the indecisive General Election of Thursday, 6th May 2010. The source used was http://www.sabian.org/Alice/lgchap04.htm

TWO LOVELY CATS

Two lovely cats
Sleeping in our living room
One on a pouffée
The other on a settee

What do they think about?
Birds and mice?
('Mmm! That's very nice')
Or of their favourite cream?

Two lovely cats
Sleeping in our living room,
One on a pouffée
The other on a settee

Curled up balls of life
One large male, mainly white
With outstretched paw
The other a tiger-tailed, tabby female
Lightly snoring away
What are their thoughts?
What images flash across their minds?
A great black nothingness
Or nightmares of loud teenage boys
Clattering around the house

Two lovely cats
Sleeping in our living room
One on a pouffée
The other on a settee

The tabby stirs slightly
The other lightly snores
A balm for the soul
A picture of restful peace
Quietly content in silent bliss
Extra years given to one's life
Let them enjoy their dreams

Two lovely cats
Sleeping in our living room
One on a pouffée
The other on a settee

But at three in the morning
It's howl, scratch and growl,
The cats are on the prowl
A patter of paws
An ear shattering screech
Something muttered about *two loathsome animals*'
And *'Do we have to have them?'*
A creaking bedroom door opening
The sound of angry human steps
(*'Are they mine?'*)
Thumping down the staircase
The fumbled unlocking of a door
A cry of *"Go! Go! I'm sick of you!"*
Another tired sigh
A clash of a metal gate
Slow heaving steps back up the stairs
I clamber back into bed
Hearing my wife
Grumbling about my failure
To be firm with those animals
In response
I soon fall asleep
Oblivious to the
Two feline horrors
Thrown out into
A frost-caked night

Two lovely cats
Sleeping in our living room
One on a pouffée
The other on a settee

But early in the morning,
It's a very different story![100]

---

[100] This poem was written on Tuesday, 9th December 2003. Its theme expresses the joyful exasperation of cat ownership.

TYPHOON TIDAL WAVE

A typhoon tidal wave
Roars noisily in
Smashing, sweeping, shattering
All before it
Upending the fragile vessels of men
Flooding a beach of many pleasures
Surging forever onward
Overturning the homes
Of once soundly sleeping inhabitants
Ending their lives in
A polluted watery grave
Defiling formerly fertile fields
With a dirty layer of mud
Dumping debris
With casual contempt

No compassion is known
No mercy is shown
As it rushes relentlessly onwards
Across flat plains
Criss-crossed by meandering roads
Breaking only when it comes to
Rock flanked hills;
Suddenly, it ebbs
Leaving the broken mannequins
Of humanity behind
Soon, only the stench is left[101]

---

[101] This meditation was written on Monday, 19th May 2008 in response to disastrous cyclonic floods in Southern Burma.

UNWANTED COMPLIMENTS

My darling
My dear
My love

What do you mean *'It sounds false?'*

My cuddly bunny girl
My furry teddy bear
My sweet pussycat

Why do you say *'It sounds silly?'*

My cute angel
My delectable Mata-Hari
My tempting Delilah

You say *'It's ridiculous!'*

Fairest of the fair
Light of my eyes
Seducer of my soul

Can't a man express affection to his wife after years of happy marriage?

Foo-foo
Goo-goo
Moo-moo

'Wham!' you've struck me with a pillow

On mum!
Lovely mother!
Ma-ma!

You shout *'I am not your mother!'*

Let me try something in the poetical vein –
'Your gravy brown eyes
Are like two muddy puddles
Filling up with heavenly rain'

Slam! You've shut the bedroom door

Now at last I can read my book in peace.[102]

---

[102] This poem was written on Saturday, May 24th 2003 and expresses the playful childishness which can feature in married life.

WAS IT?

Was it six years ago when I
Heaved one of the biggest sighs of relief in my life?

Was it six years ago when I
Wandered a University Campus, punching the air and yelling
'blooming marvellous?'

Was it six years ago when I
Gave the nice ladies who did my word-processing a fizzy bottle of champagne?

Was it six years ago when I
Visited my wife at work, excitedly informing her of a delightful development?

Was it six years ago when I
Rang family members and told them the same news

Was it six years ago when I
Began to see new opportunities mushrooming in my career?

Was it really June 19th 1998 when I
First heard that I had passed the Post Graduate Certificate in Education?[103]

---

[103] This meditation was written at a student's house on Friday, 18th June 2004. Its theme is the need to rejoice in (and draw comfort from) past successes.

WEDLOCK HEMLOCK

How wearily time passes in dreary wedlock
Twenty long years have ground slowly by
Why did I ever catch your roving eye?
I hate being trapped in marital deadlock
Being with you is like drinking hemlock
Oh how I bitterly sigh to die
Yet still your cold blue eyes are dry
From the very start it was gridlock
We were deceived by youthful passion
Marital boredom soon set in
Over many long years we grew apart
Amidst our children's boisterous din
Now that divorce is an acceptable fashion
Let's quickly make a new start
Be honest! I never was in your heart[104]

---

[104] This meditation was written on Thursday, 5th August 2004 and expresses the bitterness resulting from a broken marriage.

WHAT DO I SEE?

What do I see before my eyes?

Black letters and mathematical symbols performing a ballet dance

What do I see before my eyes?

Letters and symbols arranging into a formula

What do I see before my eyes?

A hidden reality being unveiled

What do I see before my eyes?[105]

The equation $E = MC^2$

---

[105] This meditation was written at a certain hospital cafeteria on Friday, 8th October 2004 whilst the author was going through an exceptionally creative period in his life. Its theme is the mystery and wonder of the creative process.

WHAT DO WOMEN WANT?

'What do women want?'
Was the question posed by Sigmund Freud
To the outrage of many feminists:
After thirty years of marriage
To the best woman in the world
I've now come-up with some provisional answers

Women want tender loving care
They long for comfort, intimacy and sympathy
For all their endless problems
They crave to have your child
To have your new life
Kicking inside them
They want to be special
To be your unique centre of attention
They long to be pleased with
All manner of little gifts
(Never tell them how much they cost)

They also want you to listen with endless patience
To their unlimited number of anxieties
Concerning health, clothes and relationship problems –
They even want you to switch off
Your favourite television programme
So you can hear their tales of woe

If this should happen late at night
And you chance to fall asleep
(And even worse snore)
Then expect a good kicking
To awaken you to hear
Their unceasing torrent of sorrow

In short, what women want
Is a constant supply of love –

As for the question
'What makes women happy?'
Give me another thirty years of marriage
And I just might come-up with
A very tentative answer[106]

---

[106] This meditation was written on Friday 15th May 2009 when my wife's anxiety provoked the question that opens this poem.

WHAT USE?

What use were our labours?
What use were our savings?
What use was all our prudent care?

Now our labour is unwanted
Now our savings have all but gone
Now our bills are left unpaid

Like an overheated boiler our worries bubble away
Like an army of locusts our worries devour us
Like a gnawing cancer our worries make us ill

Filling us with perplexity
Filling us with fear
Filling us with a paralysing panic

No work is available
No jobs are to be had
No employment is to be found

Now –

Only the misery of empty days is left
Only the humiliation of unemployment is preserved
Only the fragile husk of outward dignity remains

Is there any hope left?
Is there any joy remaining?
Is there any future for us or for our children?

See the milling queues at the Job Centres
See the haunted, gaunt faces scanning the Job Ads
See the dismay of those anxiously completing Job Application
Forms

Those in work fear the redundancy notice
Those with houses fear the re-possession order
Those with businesses are terrified of bankruptcy

Our favourite retail outlets are closing down
Our shopping malls have many boarded-up premises
Our purchases now take place in local charity shops

Now –

All hope is gone
All joy has departed
All plans have been thwarted

We exist only for the moment
We struggle on from day to day
We do our best with what little we have

These are the days of financial meltdown
These are the days of the *'credit crunch'*
These are the days we never dreamed we'd see

Days in which our lives are blighted
Days in which our debts multiply
Days in which our mental and physical health begin to fail

At night we lie awake brooding
At night we toss and turn in worry
At night the very real nightmare of destitution haunts us

Can we do anything?
Can politicians do anything?
Can anyone do anything?

Now –

Experts say *'the situation is complicated'*
Experts say *'solutions are difficult to find'*
Experts say *'no agreed remedy exists'*

Politicians offer conflicting promises
Politicians make contradictory predictions
Politicians change their rhetoric from day to day

Lacking is any sense of vision
Lacking is any sense of leadership
Lacking is any sense of steady direction

Where can we go?
Where can we find rest?
Where can we find real hope?

Everything has turned to dust
Everything has fallen into ruin
Everything has ended in total failure

Now –

Nothing remains but empty pockets
And the inner hollow echo of hopeless despair[107]

---

[107] This poem was written on Friday, 23rd January 2009 and can be viewed as a sequel to *'Meltdown.'* It explores the link between a universal economic and a personal, emotionally felt, depression.

WHEN HE WAS BORN

The afternoon when my grandson was born
I was caught napping and dreaming in bed
Suddenly awakened by a loud car horn
My heart was quickly filled with a fearful dread

The *'nipper'* was ever so much like his dad –
With his mum in full post-natal bloom;
Their joy, they told me, near drove both quite mad
With their excitement launching them *'over the moon!'*
I may not have heard that first lusty howl
But still felt glad I hadn't missed all that day
As baby was wrapped in a clean white towel
When told, I too had echoed their *'Hooray!'*
Baby and mother then were left in peace alone –
She captivated with the wonderful new life she could own[108]

---

[108] This attempt at a Shakespearian Sonnet was written on Saturday 25th July 2009 in order to celebrate the safe arrival of our grandson who was born weighing 7ib 2oz at 3.08pm on Thursday 23rd July 2009. It was produced in collaboration with two other poets whose assistance is gratefully acknowledged.

WHO ARE THOSE MEN?

Who are those men
With long sombre faces
Parading gloomily around
A luxury hotel conference room
Holding aloft black-framed placards, stating

'The end is nigh!'
'Prepare to meet thy doom!'
'It's all finished!'
'There's no hope!'
'We're all stuffed!'

Are they religious cranks
Preparing for a rally?
Are they actors rehearsing for a drama?
Are they some sort of protest group?

No, they're economists and bankers
With nothing else to do
Because they're trapped inside a hotel building
By a harsh Scandinavian Winter
In the middle of a global credit crunch[109]

---

[109] This poem was written on Wednesday, 12th February 2009.

WIFE LIFE

May God bless you my wife
May God grant you fresh life
May God provide you with peace
So your headaches will cease

May you accept His will
May you enjoy His fill
May you be His pet
No longer to fret

You are my great delight
You are a pretty sight
You are my sweet lover
I don't want any other[110]

---

[110] This meditation was written on Friday, 20th August 2004, just before beginning a walk with my wife around Saint Abb's Head, Southern Scotland. Its theme is how love makes one want the very best for one's partner.

WIFE! WIFE!

Wife, Wife, in a stew!

Pale old wallpaper hangs askew
Foot trapped in a small paint pot
Under the collar you grow hot
Clasped in hand a dripping brush
You were in too much of a rush
Rolled up carpet on the floor
There's no handle on the door
Out of sockets wires do hang
I only hope there is no bang!

Wife, Wife, in a stew!

I am hiding locked in the loo
Angry call you do yell
Something about *'blood and hell'*
Into the living room I timidly go
Drips of paint continue to flow
Metal ladder clatters down
On your face a furious frown
Your cheeks have flushed an angry red
Matters have come to an ugly head

Wife, Wife, in a stew!

The hands you have are too few
I pull the paint pot very hard
Its contents are thick, like lard
A hearty yank I make -
This is not a piece of cake
At last your leg wriggles free
But the pot flies past me
Into the window it does smash
We hear a most unearthly CRAAASH!

Wife, Wife, in a stew!

Your work has formed an endless queue
Steam from your ears does emit
It's all very hard I admit
From your lips comes an angry roar
Into my skull it does bore
I decide to make a quick escape
Wish I were Superman with his cape
Long to travel as fast as light
Into what is a desperate flight!

Wife, Wife, in a stew!

There's nothing I can do
Out to work I must flee
No time to hear your desperate plea
Yes, I am hopeless! Yes, I am useless!
Yes, I've left a mess, nothing less!
Must go or I'll be late
Won't expect a meal on a plate
Ta-Ta my love!
No need to give me a shove

Wife, Wife, in a stew!

I close the back door; sighing *'phew!'* [111]

---

[111] This piece was written on Saturday, June 7th 2003, whilst travelling by bus from Central Manchester to Didsbury. Earlier that day, I had left my wife decorating the living room of our house. It explores the disastrous situations which may arise when undertaking interior decoration.

WINTER TRAFFIC

Like metal beetles
With luminous, electric eyes
A line of cars grind their way forward –
Wheels noisily spinning on a slushy, ice-caked road;
Grinding, grinding their way forward
To nowhere
On a cold and misty winter's morning[112]

WIT

There was a pupil of no wit
Who gave his teachers such a fit
Gormless he forever would sit
Of homework he did not a bit
Nor ever any sign of gym kit
Other pupils he would hit
Or at best yell at them, *'you nit!'*
Me he loved to call *'a git'*
He really was the lowest pit
Am I also losing my wit?[113]

---

[112] This poem was written on Monday, 11th January 2010 in very wintry conditions. It was inspired by watching a traffic jam from my bedroom window.
[113] This ditty was written at a student's house on Friday, 11th June 2004. It expresses the exasperation of teaching difficult children.

YOU ARE

You are the best
Compassion is your garment
Gentleness your robe
A quiet goodness your trade mark
Kind as a wife
Patient as a mother
A proof reader beyond compare
Should anything happen to me
Please respect my memory
By harbouring no regrets and
Considering our marriage a great success
There's nothing more to say except
'I love you!'[114]

EPILOGUE: NEW THINGS

Now it's time to go
This show is drawing to an end
I hope it's not been too much of a blow
Thank you for seeking
Thank you for reading
Thank you for heeding
So let things be
Goodbye from me[115]

---

[114] This poem was written on Wednesday, June 4th 2003 nineteen days before our twenty-fourth wedding anniversary. It expresses the warm love which can exist in marriage.

[115] This poem was written on Thursday, June 5th 2003. Its theme is the need to let poetry help one see things in a new light.

160

PART B: FOUR SEASONS

(Poems about Different Times of the Year)

PRELUDE: SOMETHING FOR ALL SEASONS

If it's not winter cold sores
Its summer heat stroke

If it's not winter bronchitis
Its summer asthma

If it's not winter flu
Its summer sickness

If it's not winter gloom
Its summer storms

If it's not winter revellers
Its summer lager louts.

If it's not winter heating bills
Its summer holiday expenses

If it's not winter difficulty
Its summer nuisance

There's always something
For all seasons[116]

---

[116] This piece was written on Tuesday, 27th April 2004 and expresses the way every part of the year has its own problems.

DYING AUTUMN

Autumn!
The season of sweet smelling decay

Autumn!
The season of drooping multi-coloured leaves

Autumn!
The season of Indian summer-light

Autumn!
The season of damp clammy mists

Autumn!
The season of cold torrential rain

Autumn!
The season of lengthening dark evenings

Autumn!
The season of pungent garden fires

Autumn!
The season of brown stubble fields

Autumn!
The season of thick woolly jumpers

Autumn!
The season of loud firework noises

Autumn!
The season of fading splendour
Yet full of enjoyment and beauty[117]

---

[117] This piece was written on Thursday 15th July 2010 whilst suffering from hay fever.

GRIDLOCK WINTER

Part 1

I saw a nation near total collapse
...near total collapse[118]

Arctic winds blew hard from Northern Siberia
...from Northern Siberia

Dropping a white blizzard shroud
...white blizzard shroud

Gridlocked roads were covered in wet slushy ice
...wet slushy ice

Trapping motorists, needing rescuing by hard-pressed police
...by hard-pressed police

Having to spend the night in cramped overnight shelters
...cramped overnight shelters

---

[118] Performers may encourage the audience to repeat this echo in order to increase a sense of participation

Part 2

Many city and country schools had to remain closed all day
...closed all day

A February ice age having halted our transport system
...our transport system

Shivering TV reporters covering the scene from gale-blown motorway bridges
...gale-blown motorway bridges

Gently mocked by colleagues reporting from snug, warm studios
... snug, warm studios

Laughing children eagerly throwing white balls of snow
...balls of snow

Their play marking a return to lost childhood innocence
...lost childhood innocence

Four guilty bankers grovelling before a parliamentary *'Select Committee'*
...parliamentary *'Select Committee'*

Their self-serving apologies so utterly meaningless
...so utterly meaningless

Their negligent folly having brought a bitter economic freeze
...bitter economic freeze

Gloomy economists trapped by inclement weather inside an ice-bound Oslo Hotel
...ice-bound Oslo Hotel

Along with bankers, analysing a global financial crisis
...global financial crisis

But unable to make a decision concerning any possible remedy
...any possible remedy

Part 3

Newly unemployed looking for jobs that no longer exist
...no longer exist

Their mortgage payments already badly in arrears
...badly in arrears

No longer able to afford basic necessities
...afford basic necessities

Will this economic winter ever come to an end?
...to an end?

Which one of us can hope to answer this question?
...answer this question?

All the relevant indicators show a serious decline
...a serious decline

Financial reporters gleefully state how bad everything is
...bad everything is

The whole world banking system is near total collapse
...near total collapse

Having caused Britain's bitterly hard gridlocked winter
...hard gridlocked winter[119]

---

[119] This poem was written on Wednesday, 12th February 2009 when severe icy weather had coincided with a worsening in the *'economic climate.'* The harsh weather conditions described here re-occurred with even greater ferocity in December 2010.

RESURRECTION SPRING

Healing spring sunlight
Hallows an old poet's stomping ground
With glistening, glittering, golden beams
Eagerly provoking an
Easter resurrection of plant life

Woolly sun-shimmered clouds
Drift lazily over
A bracken-strewn moorland ridge
That looms like a petrified wave
Over the sooty terraced houses of
Mytholmroyd village
Tucked sleepily in the valley below

Once a future Poet Laureate
Had played there
Feeding an imagination
That would express itself
In the poems I was
Forced to study at school
Each one portraying nature
As something bleak, savage and cruel
An arena of death for many an animal

But now a thousand sunshine daffodils greet me
Providing testimony of new life
As I tenderly squeeze the hand of the woman I love

A muffled roar of traffic
Drifts up the valley side
Amidst the bleat of new born lambs
Each noisily proclaiming
This is Easter time,
The occasion for new life and fresh hope!'
Birds circle overhead
Providing their own gentle greeting
The faint tangy scent of moss
Confirms the natural scene

A stile lies ahead
The first of many to clamber over
The squeak of an opening gate
A climb over a slippery wooden ladder
One last glance thrown back to Mytholmroyd
Then up into muddy woodland
As gently laboured breathing
Marks the beginning of a long walk to Hebden Bridge[120]

---

[120] This poem was written on Sunday 12th April 2009. It first came to mind whilst standing with my wife above some rocks overlooking Mytholmroyd village – the birthplace of the poet Ted Hughes (1930-1998) whose work was standard reading for English GCE classes during the early 1970s. Chiefly remembered for his ability to attract self-destructive women, Ted Hughes held the position of Poet Laureate from 1984 until his death. Although only the first six years of his life had been spent in Mytholmtoyd its location helped to inspire his subsequent poetry.

SPURN HEAD SUMMER

Hot summer
Late June weather
Warm breeze

Flat horizon
A remote location
Lost villages

Kilnsea Farms
Roadside hedgerows
Swaying trees

Shifting sands
Curving peninsula
A coastal breeze

Chirping birds
Crunching pebbles
An insect hums

Aching back
Baking hot feet
Cooling breeze

Sewerage stench
Mudflat smells
Sweaty odour

Parched mouth
Dry cactus tongue
Liquid relief

Clearing lungs
Unclogged airways
Easy breathing

Advancing waters
Retreating shoreline
Rising sea

Nibbling tides
Falling mud cliffs
Crumbling clay

Rotting groins
Flood swept cottages
Broken walls

Old bunkers
Wartime ruins
New debris

Narrow path
Slow passing vehicles
Distant views

Tidal marshes
Brown mudflats
Protected wildlife

Creeping dunes
Crunching Seaweed
Needle grass

Rocky beach
Engraved fossils
Broken jetties

Peeling paint
Abandoned lighthouse
Shut entrance

Strong currents
A long, high jetty
A ship's wake

A lifeboat
One brave crew
Saved lives

Closed cafe
Ugly radio station
Bobbing ferry

Estuary view
Old fortification
Lapping waves

Sandy spit
Flanking waters
Estuary border

Cruising boats
A standing oil rig
Grimsby view

Welcome rest
A consumed snack
Refreshing drinks

Faint feeling
A sunshine doze
Perfect rest

Unusual beauty
Now a memory
On this paper[121]

---

[121] This poem was written on Monday 28th June 2010 after having enjoyed an excellent walk (with my wife) around Spurn Head Peninsula. We'd been staying at Kilnsea (East Yorkshire) celebrating our thirty-first Wedding Anniversary.

POSTLUDE: SEASONAL RELAXATION

Between two dunes we lie
Outstretched
Heads resting upon rucksacks
Gazing dreamily upon the sea and sand
When not glancing at each other

Its mid-summer
We natter lazily about small things
About the times we were courting
About those we knew in our youth
About how we met over 30 years ago
Then silence
Except for the noise of
A swishing-swashing, surging sea
No need to speak
Our quiet love is worth a thousand voices
Not even the sonic boom
Of a distant RAF jet can disturb
Our silent reveries[122]

---

[122] This poem was written on Wednesday 30th June 2010 the day after returning home from Humberside. It's based upon memories of the picnic-lunch stops we enjoyed at Spurn head and lying on the beach at Easington (East Yorkshire).

PART C: LOOPY LIMERICKS[123]

---

[123] This collection of Limericks was written from Thursday, 8th October-Tuesday, 13th October 2009 in response to a stimulating workshop given at the Ilkley Literary Festival during the first of these dates.

1) CAT LIMERICKS

1.

There was an old cat of Leeds
Who would vex us with his deeds
So very naughty was he
'Cos on our floor he would pee
So relieving his bodily needs

There is an old cat called *'Ziggy'*
In shape he's a bit like Twiggy
Sitting all day on the bin
Creating a loud, frightful din
Until he gets fed like a piggy

Once a jet black cat bit my nose
While I lay in bed in a doze[124]
I shouted *'go away!'*
But he decided to stay
Now he's starting to nibble my toes

Here's a cat called *'Banker'*
Who looks like a tanker
Your money he'll thieve
Then he'll leave you to grieve
His schemes are nothing but canker

2.

There once was a cat who sat on my face
Who purred on and on at such a fast pace
He then did a whiff
I nearly went stiff
Before hurtling him into outer space[125]

---

[124] This actually happened on Saturday, 10th October 2009, when a thin black cat from a neighbour's house jumped onto my bed seeking attention. My nose was sore for a while afterwards. On Friday, 6th November 2009 he bit my large toe whilst I was lying on top of the bed, reading.
[125] This poem was written on Friday, 19th February 2010 and was based upon a real incident that had happened at 6.30am that morning.

2) LIMERICKS ON WALKING & WALKERS

There once was a man from Kent
Who wanted to climb Penny-Ghent[126]
When he finally ascended
A fog descended
And into a deep bog he went

There once was a lady called Chalker
Who loved nothing but hiking in Majorca
Country rambling was her game
But she could be a pain
'Cos she really was an endless talker

Judy was always moody
Over nothing she'd grow broody
I said *'let things be*
Don't get at me'
So now, I go walking with Trudy

The queen was walking at Gleneagle
In manner o' so regal
The press hovered round
The queen went to ground
Before things began to get nasty *'n'* legal

---

[126] A peak in the Yorkshire Dales

3) PARTY CONFERENCE LIMERICKS

Tony Blair's grand photo-call
Was held in a large imposing hall
He flashed his Bambi smile
As was his usual style
In Europe, he wants to walk tall

Gordon Brown's photo call
Very soon began to pall
A big great hulk
He would visibly sulk
He's heading for a really big fall

There once was a Blair clone called *'Cameron'*
Who really was a great podgy *'Shameron'*
'Oh, just call me Dave,
Your country I'll save'
But please just let me *'yammer-on'*

In weak contrast is George Osborne
On Europe he refused to be drawn
The city thought him a boy
Refusing to buy him a toy
Media Jackals view him with utter scorn

Here's a lightweight called Clegg
For your votes he'll most often beg
On *'telly'* he looks rather dim
No one can recognize him
Except an old lady called Meg

In strong contrast is Vince Cable
Who wants to make all things stable
The financial crash he foresaw
Credit couldn't continue to soar
But still nothing remains on the table

4) FORGOTTEN BIRTHDAY

My wife had a birthday to celebrate
But no one could remember the date
Ben 'er son asked *'When?'*
His dad retorted *'Is it then?'*
Grrr! The pair she'd love to decimate

Her friend *'Ol' Little-legs'* came around
Fussing and sniffing like a bloodhound
I'm here my dear
So do not fear!'
She said with a loud raucous sound

For a generous birthday tea she came
But *'Little-legs'* had no sense of shame
Biscuits she really loved to munch
With a loud, noisy crunch
Her appetite she just couldn't tame

Hot tea the two ladies slurped
Before each gave a great loud burp
They nattered away
As I stayed away
My wife's birthday I wanted to shirk

At last, her birthday came to an end
It almost drove me round the bend
A card I forgot
A slap was my lot
And no gift did I bother to send![127]

---

[127] This limericks was written in my bedroom on the morning of Tuesday, 22nd December 2009 on the occasion of my wife's fifty-third birthday, which I had *'almost'* forgotten.

PART D: THE SILVER POEMS

(Three Poems Celebrating our Silver Wedding Anniversary on Wednesday, 23rd June 2004)[128]

---

[128] The following three poems were written on Monday, 28th June 2004, at the close of our Silver Wedding Anniversary celebrations. I sat jotting things down whilst my wife had a nap next to me, lying on a park bench behind the greenhouse at Jephson Gardens, Leamington Spa. (They first began to emerge during the previous day, whilst seated at the garden of *'Hall's Place,'* Stratford upon Avon.)

RETURNING MEMORIES

When I see you lying there
Dozing peacefully on a park bench
Memories return of the time
You processed down the aisle
In all your white finery
The centre of attention
From admiring friends and family

At that time
You were a rosy cheeked girl
With tinted glasses
And jet black hair
Curled into a perm
You looked
So hopeful
So innocent
So vulnerable
Like a well iced cake
Ready to be eaten

Now you are older
Your cheeks are still rosy
But your short straight hair
Has streaks of grey
Curving above your ears and
There's often a look of worry
In your face
As you try to battle
A multitude of anxieties

Yet I still see the girl within you and
I love both her and
The mature woman
She has now become

STRANGE MYSTERY

As you sleep gently
On that park bench
At Leamington Spa
I look back
One quarter of a century, pondering

*'What strange mystery enabled our marriage to survive
Four distracting children
Interfering outsiders
Serious financial shortages
Messy work situations
Not to mention your eternal headaches
My endless capacity to lose things
And the grotesque decadence of our society?'*

The mystery of what makes a marriage work
Is too profound for me to explore
On a hot and sunny afternoon;
All I can do for now
Is rest and be thankful
For its success

TWENTY-FIVE

Twenty-Five Years of marriage have passed
      And
Still you delight me with your presence

Twenty-Five Years of marriage have passed
      And
Still you look pretty before my eyes

Twenty-Five Years of marriage have passed
      And
Still you arouse a warm glowing feeling within me

Twenty-Five Years of marriage have passed
      And
Still you inspire a daft playfulness in me

Twenty-Five Years of marriage have passed
      And
Still you make me laugh and chuckle

Twenty-Five Years of marriage have passed
      And
Still you prompt me to call you silly names

Twenty-Five Years of marriage have passed
      And
Still you provoke me to cuddle you

Twenty-Five Years of marriage have passed
      And
Still you incite me to many loud kisses

Twenty-Five Years of marriage have passed
    And
Still you gain my admiration for who you are

Twenty-Five Years of marriage have passed
    And
Still you are my very best and only true friend

Twenty-Five Years of marriage have passed
    And
Still you create in me many tender feelings towards you

Twenty-Five Years of marriage have passed
    And
Still you are the dearest of companions

Twenty-Five Years of marriage have passed
    And
Still you hold my hand when we walk out together

Twenty-Five Years of marriage have passed
    And
Still you retain that charming *'Geordie'* accent

Twenty-Five Years of marriage have passed
    And
Still you are kind, selfless and caring

Twenty-Five Years of marriage have passed
    And
Still you represent the *'better half'*

Twenty-Five Years of marriage have passed
    And
Still you charm me with your funny ways

Twenty-Five Years of marriage have passed
    And
Still you gently calm my ruffled nerves

Twenty-Five Years of marriage have passed
      And
Still you display a patient forbearance

Twenty-Five Years of marriage have passed
      And
Still you skilfully organise my daily life

Twenty-Five Years of marriage have passed
      And
Still you personify goodness, kindness and compassion

Twenty-Five Years of marriage have passed
      And
Still you manage our money very well

Twenty-Five Years of marriage have passed
      And
Still you are well organised and practical

Twenty-Five Years of marriage have passed
      And
Still you can be full of fun and joy

Twenty-Five Years of marriage have passed
      And
Still you are mine and I am yours forever

PART C:
WITH LOVE TO PENELOPE

(A range of poems dedicated to our stillborn Grand-daughter
Penelope Jemima)

LAMENT FOR PENELOPE

I don't know you my little one
I will never hold you in my arms
Or enjoy seeing you grow
From infancy to adulthood

Not for you holidays in Scarborough
Help with your homework
Or noisy sleepovers with your friends
Death has stolen our joy

No one can count the number of your days
Or blow the candles out on your birthday cake
For your candle was blown out
Whilst you still resided in your mother's womb

You will never see the light of day
Nor hear your mother's cooing voice
You will not see the proud smile on your father's face
Or be fussed over by doting grandparents

In your death may there be new life
In your end may there be a fresh beginning
May this affliction turn into a blessing
And in suffering may redemption be found

But farewell my little Penelope
Whose life on earth has been cut short
But may you live on through words
You helped inspire[129]

---

[129] This meditation was written on Friday, 14th March 2008 the morning after the writer had heard about the death of his granddaughter, Penelope Jemima, whose heart had ceased beating in her mother's womb.

STILL BEAUTY

What still beauty is lying there
Cradled in the arms of a silently weeping mother?
How perfectly formed you are
With your tufts of black hair
Small nose
Large toes
And puckered baby mouth
That emits no cry

You are my love, the very personification of perfection
The only thing you lack is life itself

Playing with your fingers and toes
Is my grandfather's delight
How I wish there was some grip in them
How I yearn for some recognition
From your gently closed eyes

At anytime you look as if you could awaken
And begin cooing as all babies do
But sadly your sleep continues still

But for this brief moment, let me enjoy the company
Of my dear, dear granddaughter[130]

---

[130] This meditation was written on Monday, 17th March 2008, the day after the writer and his wife had visited their stillborn granddaughter, Penelope Jemima, in a hospital side room as she lay cradled in her parents' arms.

FAREWELL

Farewell my lovely, farewell
Farewell my granddaughter, farewell
Farewell my poppet, farewell

Farewell to a mother's loving embrace
Farewell to a father's tears
Farewell to all the world and its cares

Farewell Penelope Jemima
Seeing and playing with you was great
But you're in good hands now[131]

---

[131] This meditation was written on Monday, 17th March 2008, the day after the writer and his wife had visited their stillborn granddaughter, Penelope Jemima, in a hospital side room as she was being cradled in her parents' arms.

COMFORT

She is in the hands of God –
In the hands of the living God
Who brings good out of sorrow

She is enjoying unlimited care –
Unlimited care from her Heavenly Father
Who has called her to Himself

She is blest with boundless joy –
With boundless joy from Christ her friend
Who is her wise Protector

She is being filled with endless peace –
With endless peace from the Spirit of God
Who brings her wholeness

She is at rest with the angels in heaven –
At rest with the singing angels
Who rejoice in her salvation

She is being greatly blest –
Greatly blest by the awesome love of God
Which was received quietly and without struggle[132]

---

[132] This meditation was written on Monday, 17th March 2008, the day after the writer and his wife had visited their stillborn granddaughter, Penelope Jemima, in a hospital side room as she was being cradled in her parent's arms.

TURMOIL-ON-THE-BOIL

I *'dunno'* what to do
It's all so cruel
My heart's filled with dismay
I *'dunno'* what to say

Turmoil-On-The-Boil

A new life was to be born
Now all we can do is mourn
It's all very sad
Am I going mad?

Turmoil-On-The-Boil

She is a beautiful sight
But things didn't go right
In our heart-torn sorrow
There's no tomorrow

Turmoil-On-The-Boil

Everyone's in a state
At this cruel blow of fate
There's been much pain
Where is the gain?

Turmoil-On-The-Boil

Thoughts pour through my brain
Like a monsoon rain
Images dart around
Words make no sound

Turmoil-On-The-Boil

Poetry fills my head
As I lie in bed
Got to write it down
My brow furrowed in a frown

Turmoil-On-The-Boil

On lined paper I leave my mark
My words look very stark
Lines and verses written out
Only wish I could howl and shout

Turmoil-On-The-Boil

Can only live for now
Don't tell me how
Got these tasks to finish
Grief doesn't diminish

Turmoil-On-The-Boil

Deal with this trial
Avoid any bile
Must recover fast
Nerves ready for a funeral repast

Turmoil-On-The-Boil

Long with my heart
That we didn't have to part
Buried in the ground
In our hearts you are found

Turmoil-On-The-Boil

Like a Gamma Ray Burst you came
Our lives will not remain the same
You shone with a brilliant light
Before fading into death's dark night[133]

Turmoil-On-The-Boil

(Pause, repeat and fade the chorus)[134]

---

[133] On Wednesday, March 19,th *"A gigantic stellar explosion....shattered the record for the furthest object visible with the naked eye, scientists say* – [at 7.5 billion years] *halfway across the whole universe,"* (World Science, Thursday, 20th March 2008, http://www.world-science.net/othernews/080320_grb)

[134] This meditation was written late in the evening of Tuesday, 18th March 2008 and further amended Saturday 22nd March to add the verse about the Gamma Ray Burst. It expresses the mental turmoil felt by the writer following the unexpected stillbirth of his granddaughter, Penelope Jemima.

WHERE?

Where are you going my lovely, my lovely
Where are you going my love?
Up into a place
That's very safe
That's where you're going my love.

Where are you going my lovely, my lovely
Where are you going my love?
Up into a life
Without any strife
That's where you're going my love.

Where are you going my lovely, my lovely
Where are you going my love?
Up into a place
Where peace will never cease
That's where you're going my love.

Yet here, will I miss you my lovely, my lovely
Yes here, will I miss you my love
From my grief-torn heart
You will never depart
That's where you are my love, my love
That's where you are, my love[135]

---

[135] This poem was written late in the evening of Thursday, 20th March 2008, the day before the funeral of the writer's stillborn granddaughter, Penelope Jemima. It first emerged whilst the writer was swimming on his back at a local Leisure Centre.

As

As the stars twinkle in the heavens
So shall your light shine in our lives

As a rainbow shimmers in the evening sky
So shall your beauty remain in our eyes

As the rays of a sinking sun play around the shadows
So shall your loveliness remain a cherished memory[136]

---

[136] This poem was written late in the evening of Thursday, 20th March 2008, the day before the funeral of the writer's stillborn granddaughter, Penelope Jemima. It first emerged whilst the writer was swimming at a local Leisure Centre.

GUSTING HEAVENWARDS

Terrible news
Penelope is gone
Bewildered sorrow

Creative surge
Poems written on paper
Written in tears

Distressed parents
Much crying and weeping
Hopes all dashed

Delicate rain
Cold wind blowing
Weeping skyline

Poetry recited
Fumbling tributes paid
Choking silence

Coffin let down
Roses gently thrown in
Time for goodbyes

Balloons released
Bobbing gently along
Past the trees

Time to depart
Black garbed mourners
Slowly leave

Pink balloons
Caught gusting upwards
Up to the clouds

Rushing to join
Penelope Jemima
Up in the heavens[137]

HOPE

Hope in the truth
It will set you free

Hope in divine grace
It is freely available

Hope in divine mercy
It is to be enjoyed

Hope in divine love
It can be received

Hope in the resurrection
It will certainly happen

Hope in a glorious re-union
With the loved one we lost[138]

---

[137] This cycle of Japanese Haikus was written on Saturday 22nd March 2008 the morning after the funeral of Penelope Jemima.
[138] This meditation was written on Easter Sunday, 23rd March 2008 just before my wife and I set out for an Easter Communion service at church.

TRAIN CARRIAGE DOZE

Sponge-squeezed dry,
Cloth rung out
Creative inspiration now flagging
As a bitter grief ebbs slowly away

Time to visit the country
And escape everything

Eyelids flutter closed
Cloudy thoughts swirl around my brain
Train carriage rocks gently
As I slip into a doze

Time to have a good moorland walk
To restore my grief-bruised soul

Eyes now firmly shut
Discordant thoughts falter and fade away
Train line clatter quietens down
There is no longer any poetry in me[139]

---

[139] This meditation was written on Easter Monday, 24th March 2008, after the writer had awoken from a light doze whilst travelling by train for a day out in the country. It expresses the exhaustion he felt following a major period of creativity.

PART F: SHORT STORIES

A PATCH OF GREEN

At the side of our block of 1960s terraced flats lies a small patch of green. To be honest, it's not very impressive – just a raised grassy area, curving around like a leaning number nine towards a small adjoining car park. Lying near its centre is a rectangular section of paving stones – the last remains of a former greenhouse. Even now a mantle of grass is slowly advancing over them, attempting to hide their very existence. The whole area is bounded on one side by a low crumbling wall, valiantly trying to separate the green from the cracked and gritty surface of the car park. The grass gradually peters out in favour of a small densely wooded area, sited on the top of a steep rail embankment. Lying at its base are the gleaming rail tracks, leading directly to the smoke-caked mouth of a beautifully sculptured Victorian tunnel. On weekdays commuter trains regularly clatter by, full of city workers, university students and others shopping for bargains in the City Centre. Lively birdsong fills the gaps between these precisely timed and noisy interludes.

A rickety fence lines the far side of the green, its wooden stakes pointing defiantly to the sky. Blackberry bushes and bindweed constantly threaten to cover the fence in a jungle of twisting branches and leaves. Sited behind it are neatly kept allotments, stretching away as far as the eye can see. The fence carries on toward a concrete staircase leading to the flats above; and it's at this point where the tangle of branches drops away, revealing a perfect climbing frame for the local cat life. The fence turns once more, butting against the overgrown back garden of a semi-detached council house. This is where the drunken Irishman *'Paddy'* McFuddle lives. You can often hear him singing and swearing at the top of his voice. It then narrows again into another rectangular patch, passing a couple of trees and a wooden garden shed until it reaches the tree-lined road of Kingsway Drive.

Nothing much ever happens on *'the green.'* The local cats use it as a toilet-cum-play area, whilst any birds daring to land upon it quickly fly off again, after spotting a sleek furry body in the undergrowth. Summer sees the occasional visit of an obsessive black-berry picker, but for the main part our green escapes human visitation. That is, until last winter when there was a spot of bother with some delivery men. On what had been a damp and misty morning, they'd been carrying a neighbour's new plasma television. Somehow they'd managed to slip on some slushy snow and had dropped their precious cargo, apparently cracking the whole screen. Word got round that the owner had sought legal redress against the Delivery Company. Well, we could tell at a glance that he looked far from pleased with the compensation he'd received.

One sultry mid-summer's evening another minor drama took place. I was leaning against the railings bordering our first floor walkway and was gently calling out, *'Smitten! Smitten!* In case you don't know, Smitten is our plump grey tabby and white cat who appears to suffer from a *'Woody Allan'* type of neurosis. This would express itself in a piteous (or demanding) *'meow,'* a reproachful look or a frantic scratching on our most expensive items of furniture. Once or twice a day it was necessary to quieten his meowing *'pity-parties'* by playing what we called *the string game.'* This exasperating rigmarole involved dangling an old shoe lace or piece of string beneath his nose and then running away, making silly imitation bird noise in order for him to give chase, which he did for ten to fifteen minutes before getting bored. To further boost his non-existent confidence my wife would firmly plonk him in the middle of the green and watch him meander his fearful way back home, up the concrete steps. Sometimes he would (with an anxious shaking of his tiger-ringed tail) clamber over the fence and vanish into Paddy's overgrown garden. When that happened it would be my turn to call him back.

Well, here I was, urgently beckoning him, hoping he would soon appear. It was one of those evenings when day blends silently into night, forming a confused twilight. As darkness fell it enveloped our patch of green which then took on something of a spectral quality. The sky resembled a coat of blue-black velvet, punctuated by patches of hazy starlight. Only some dim garage lights alleviated the sombre blackness of the car park. *Smitten! Smitten!'* I called, in a weary and increasingly impatient tone. Suddenly, a bewildered feline face peered out from amongst the taller grass – bobbing up and down like a buoy on a choppy sea. *"Ah, there you are my silly animal! Now come back home – it's late!"* In nervous response Smitten scrambled over the fence. He gingerly approached the concrete steps like a naked climber facing an overhanging slope on Everest. All of a sudden he stopped dead in his tracks, his ears tense, upright and twitching slightly. He'd definitely heard something and he began to hesitantly move toward the dense woodland. *"No Smitten – no! Over here you daft moggy, otherwise you'll get lost like you did last time!"* Inattentive to my plea he stood poised, one paw raised slightly above the ground, ears twitching in a rather unconvincing, defensive hunter pose. He then sniffed the ground, trying to gain the scent of any potential menace. Inwardly, I debated whether to go down and rescue my wondering pet.

However, my hopes of a rescue quickly vanished when, from the direction of the woodland came an ominous scuffling sound and the noise of breaking twigs. Then suddenly, out darted a trio of foxes, each wearing an evil leer. (I knew they'd a den hidden away somewhere in the dense undergrowth of the embankment.) Hungrily, they dashed in Smitten's direction – whose rapid response was to dive headlong into one of the blackberry bushes by the fence. Thankfully, he'd not been their real target; what they were more interested in was the dustbin area. For a few seconds they broke off their chase in order to dance and caper, circling and making loud screeching noises as if performing some form of forbidden ritual. Finally, they made a dash for the rear dustbins, followed by a cacophony of scratching, screeching and scuffling in what appeared to be a wild Darwinian struggle for survival. A final triumphant bevy of screeches and the posse of foxes emerged with a booty of food in their mouths. One held a large chicken leg, the other a chunk of bread whilst the third could be seen savouring the delights of cold pizza. These night-time scavengers had found their prey and were gleefully prancing homeward toward their hidden den in a nocturnal victory parade. However, their triumphant procession came to an abrupt halt when, with a noisy crunching of tarmac, a *'metal predator'* swerved into the car park; its headlights glaring. They fixed on the fox with the chicken leg, pinning him down in an arc of piercing light as if he were a prisoner attempting a failed breakout. The hunters now felt as if they were the hunted and unleashed yet another chorus of unearthly screeching before quickly darting into the undergrowth. *'Bloomin' 'eck, what an infernal racket!'* protested a broad Yorkshire voice from an open bedroom window. Paddy had also been disturbed and could be heard discharging a barrage of incoherent profanities. Whether he was responding to the noise of the foxes on the green or to the imaginary foxes chewing his alcohol-pickled brain seemed of little consequence. A final salvo of cursing and the slamming of a door marked his shambling exit from the scene.

Smitten! Smitten!' The only response was silence. *'I'm going in you daft moggy and you'll have to stay out all night and there'll be no 'string game' tomorrow!'* I turned to enter my flat and behold, crouched in the dimly lit porch-way sat Smitten, covered in flecks of grass and other debris. He seemed sorrier for himself than ever. From the reproachful look in his eyes I could see that a fear of foxes could now be added to his already bulging file of neuroses. *"Ah, there you are my naughty boy. You must have crept up the other stairs."* We looked at one another in anxious appreciation. *"Well – you've certainly used up one of your nine lives this time around!"* I said as I patted him reassuringly on the head. He responded with a hurt, *'It's all your fault'* look and a very self-pitying *'meow!'* It was as if he was saying, *'You really don't know what I've been through.'* I tried to tickle him on the tummy whilst making a silly high-pitched *'eeee!'* noise but he was having none of it. In yet another of his aggrieved sulks and with a very sullen swish of his tail he padded into the kitchen to scoff his food.

Next morning the weather was damp and muggy. On the green the only trace of the previous night's caper was a chicken leg, (picked completely clean) lying beside the crumbling wall. The foxes had gone but their need to survive would ensure their return. Like Smitten, but in a rather different way, they'd learnt to survive by adapting to a concrete jungle created by Man.[140]

---

[140] This piece of prose was first drafted on Sunday, October 17th 2010 during a poetry workshop given at the Ilkley Literary Festival. It was substantially re-edited several times.

BAD MAN

"What was daddy like?"

"He was a bad man, your father."

So said the woman with the fist flattened face
As she protectively hovered over her daughter
Both queuing in front of a harbour-side
Ice cream stall

"But why was he bad mummy?"

"He just wasn't very nice, that's all."

Her face puckered into a frown
As a crash of violent images
Exploded inside her head

"But why?"

"He just weren't, that's all."

She shuddered
As she saw that drunken fist
Come flying towards her face
With the word *'HATE'*
Tattooed on its bruised knuckles
Oh how he'd cursed her
(It was always *'he'* or *'him'*)
She shouldn't have let him talk her out of
Leaving that women's refuge;
Her mother had always warned her that *'e war a bad sort'*
Even his own mother had thrown him out of the house
After her boyfriend had got some mates round
To sort him out;
It was the only time
She'd seen him crying
He'd turned up with two black eyes
Pleading for a place to stay

210

She'd been soft and let him in
That had been her fatal mistake

"But why mum, why?"
Asked the girl, tugging on her mother's skirt

"It's none of your business."

She said in an absent-minded way
Shuddering
As she recalled the police raid
That finally put him in jail
For assault it was said
Like a fool she'd waited for him
Hoping he'd mend his ways
Especially since she was pregnant
But he came out worse than ever
Was on the *'hard stuff'* by then
Making furtive deals
And messing around with
Low life of every sort
He'd hated the way she'd distanced herself from him
Like she was *"stuck-up'*
And much too good for him'
The beatings continued
Then there was that night
When he'd made her strip before his mates
How they'd laughed and jeered
At her humiliation
Poking her pregnant stomach
Her act being accompanied by
The thud, thud, thud of heavy rock music
The next morning she'd run off to the refuge
She'd had her baby daughter
And had even felt snatches of happiness
But he came and gave his empty promises
And like a fool she'd let him talk her out of it
But then the beatings had got even worse

"Please mum; please tell me... why are you looking at me like that – are you poorly?"

"No... Just thinkin..."

"Of what mum?"

"Oh, just nothin..."

"But mummies never just think of nothing."

About a month later
The Police had come round for one last time
He'd been found dead
His head *'kicked in'*
Down an alleyway beside *'The Old Lags'* pub
Something about a dispute over money
So they'd said
She'd been asked to identify his effects
Because his body just wasn't viewable
His death was her liberation
She knew that the night she and her daughter would be alright
He was dead;
'Good riddance to bad rubbish,'
She'd thought

"Mum"

"Shh, will yer? Now choose yer ice cream!"

She'd vowed never to mess around with men
She'd got a job as a cleaner
To make ends meet
Anything was better than staying on the dole
Where they'd *'natter on'* at you to take some *'lousy job'*
Her mother had grumbled
About having to look after *'his'* child
But then her mother had died unexpectedly
Leaving behind a bit of money
Which had paid for this holiday

212
Bringing a morsel of happiness

"Mum, I'll have that one with the big chocolate thing on!"

The ice cream was bought
It was a relief not having to worry about money
Life was bobbing along just nicely
Like *'them'* boats in the harbour

"Oh Mum!"

"Yes,"

"When will you tell me about daddy?"

"When you're ready"

"When will that be?"

"When you're older"

"But mum, I am older!"

"Just eat yer ice cream and don't pester me with them silly questions."

"But mum, you always say that!"

'And I always will!'

She retorted
Giving her daughter
A wary fond look
Gently squeezing her shoulders
And thinking
'You belong only to me now' [141]

---

[141] This poem was written on Saturday, 13th September 2008. I'd been on holiday in Falmouth in the previous August and had inadvertently overheard snatches of a conversation between a woman and her young daughter. They'd been queuing outside an Ice Cream Stall in the harbour area.

LONER

Ma name is 'ogarth Rake
Ah'm always on the make
Ah what Ah want Ah' l take[142]

From London's East End Ah came
Bitter poverty were my ball an' chain
To be a huge success were my main aim

Ma mum by ma dad got battered
'er will to live waz shattered
To 'er I were the only one 'oo mattered

Ah'd scar faced uncles oo'd worked for *'Ronnie's gang'*
Ending a good few lives with a loud *'bang!'*
'ad no conscience t' give 'em any pang

At school I were slow t' read 'n' write
But 'ad fun with many a good 'ard fight
Ah used ma fists to cause a right bloody sight

Worked for a short while on ma dad's market stall
But floggin' cheap meat soon began to pall
Runnin' a market stall really weren't a good call

Ah soon chose to join a dodgy loan shark
Ah'd collect 'is debts for 'im or else leave ma mark
(Know wot I mean?)
Owned a pit-bull with a nice threatening bark

Interest rates were 'oh so dear'
Ah got a kick out o' 'creatin' a sense o' fear
Loud thumpin' on the door would announce I waz 'ere!

Many an 'ome I would gleefully trash
All to search for a little 'ard cash
Then I'd be gone – quick as a flash!

---

[142] Performers may find it helpful to speak in an East London accent.

Dad moaned, *'You'll turn out like yer uncle Len'*
For GBH 'ed ended-up doin' seven
In Clap'am 'e used to run a big gamblin' den

Like old Len I possessed a certain charm
'e used to say *'a little smarm does no 'arm'*
Use it to prevent any sense of alarm'

A shrewd old geezer were 'e
As a youngster I'd sit on 'is knee
As 'e drank a big mug o' tea

'e told me many a grand tale
'ow on the sea 'ed used to sail
Out to defeat 'itler, without fail

Any 'ow, Ah decided to join the City
There Ah could be witty
But have no sense o' pity

A successful junk bond dealer were I
'ollered as ma shares went sky 'igh
It were all very *'do or die'*

A well known investment bank 'eadhunted me
Offered a grand six figure fee
There were no limits to my talent they could see

Savile Row suits Ah could afford to buy
A dapper little Taylor would mincingly sigh
As Ah demanded *'just one more try'*

Near the square mile I acquired a luxury home
Attended the 2,000 bash at the Millennial Dome
Who cared if the odd million or two got blown?

Shares continued to sky rocket
A nice fat bonus entered my pocket
No one would ever dare to block it

In classy brothels big financial deals were made
When 'igh on cocaine we'd often do our trade
Ah thought ma success could never ever fade

Every Russian blonde were mine
But a sultry Chinese would do just fine
Then we could do a threesome, all at one time

Wild parties in fancy castles Ah attended
With the *'in crowd'* Ah nicely blended
Didn't care 'oo Ah offended

Off Bali shores Ah went scuba divin'
Also took to fast car drivin'
Ma career waz certainly thrivin'

Poor old mum passed away
An' dad's mind began to stray
Kept whimperin' on about 'ow 'e'd loved 'er

For ma mum Ah'd done all that Ah could
But for me life was still very good
Went shootin' in a country estate wood

Then suddenly shares began to crash
From ma own *''edge fund'* were a wild dash
And ma millions went – all in a flash

The Banks 'ad made many a blunder
Our financial system were goin' under
They became an object of scornful wonder

As city institutions began to stumble
Ma own shares continued to fall an' tumble
An' ma *'creative accounts'* others began to rumble

Soon city friends abandoned me
Another failure they 'ad no wish to see
Defence lawyers charged an astronomical fee

All ma assets bled away
Ma debts were called in all on one day
On the floor of a girlfriend's flat I 'ad ter stay

Damned lawyers took the last o' ma wealth
They did that with breathtakin' stealth
Ah suffered a major breakdown in 'ealth

For multiple fraud Ah got *'done'*
Well – that were ma total crime in a sum
When sentence were passed Ah felt numb

At 'er majesty's pleasure I were detained
An' nothin' o' ma wealth were retained
Ah mean ah simply asked *"ow can I be blamed?"*

The square mile I still love to stroll
Remembering the times I were on a roll
Now ah starve on the dole

On park benches Ah fall into a restless sleep
Dreamin' o' things Ah can no longer keep
In appearance I'm a crumpled 'eap

Women now avert their gaze
As I wander in a cider-soaked 'aze
Each day's just a blurred 'ung-over daze

From waste bins Ah scavenge to eat
Beggin' can be somethin' of a feat
But why in self-pity should Ah bleat?

In my dreams Ah'm a prey to night time ghouls
Still – among the 'omeless are plenty of fools
'oo can be the most useful of tools

Despite ma impoverished pain
Am gonna defy the world an' rise again
To seize whatever crumb ah can gain

For Ah'm the city loner[143]
The city loner, Ah'm the city loner
Yeh, yeh Ah'm the le-le-loner[144]

---

[143] Performers may begin to fade here.
[144] This poem was written on Wednesday 6th January 2010 after returning home from a swim. The stuttering at the end underlines the mental and physical disintegration of the character.

RECRIMINATIONS

It was always the same dream; Every night wandering in a foggy landscape, hair dishevelled, wearing a crumpled suit and walking unsteadily on torn and wet bank notes, crying loudly, *'Where are you? Where are you?'* Then he would appear-with that fake skin tan, arms folded, standing all self-assured on a small pile of gold bullion bars. He'd be wearing a smart suit of Savile Row quality – the one reserved for state occasions – and be smiling that false friendly smile of his, eyes showing a mixture of pity and contempt.

"I'm here, Gordon – want my help do you? Dear me, this is becoming a habit."

"We're down in the opinion polls, the economy is heading into deep depression and so am I. The retail price index is up, factory gate prices are soaring, unemployment is up, government debt is spiralling out of control, the banking system has been near to collapse, a general election is looming and..."

"Spare me that meaningless treasury jargon; I had enough of it when you were chancellor."

"But Tony, I need you!"

"That was always your trouble, Gordon, you always needed me and that's why you hated me. Even before we came into office you were in denial that without me you'd be nothing – not even a treasury *'bean counter.'* I made you Gordon and I could break you – even though you are Prime Minister."

"But Tony, the Labour Party faces electoral meltdown."

"And who brought that about Gordon? If only you'd called the election the autumn after you'd schemed your way into power. At least you'd have had one full term as Prime Minister, giving time for another successor (cast in my image) to emerge."

"But Tony, I need your help."

"It's a bit too late to seek that now. When I was PM you never listened to anything I said – always blocking every proposal, always undermining my efforts to effect positive change. Your answer to every problem was to throw more money at it and to set more targets. I was surprised that the whole nation didn't grind to a halt with all the forms you gave public workers to fill in. I always knew you were too psychologically flawed to hold a really senior ministerial position."

"But you appointed me to be your successor and allowed me to be the longest serving chancellor!"

"Only because the parliamentary Labour Party wouldn't have it any other way – to keep the loyalty of our backbenchers I had to put-up with your temper tantrums, fuming sulks and endless intrigues. Anyone behaving like that in a private business would have been sacked years ago – but politics was politics and for some reason I could never fathom out why the Labour Party were in love with you. How they eagerly made you my successor without any contest! It was obvious to me – but not to our *'fraternal brothers'* – that you weren't up to the job. I could never see why they had this extraordinary confidence in you – I certainly never had, at least after the early days. I did look-up to you once because you seemed a substantial figure but I was a little naive then and that was a long, long time ago."

"They're not confident in me now. The Party would get rid of me tomorrow if they could find someone who actually wanted the job. They're letting me hang on to take the blame for this economic mess."

"Whose fault is that Gordon? Your problem was that you never knew how to really handle people – how to make yourself agreeable to them, to flatter and appeal to their vanity or to feed their hunger for *'office.'* You were just too mundane to appeal to their wishful thinking or to say what they wanted to hear. Now that was something I was always good at, *'smoozing'* was my speciality. I always took care to offer a little hope even if it was groundless. As for you, all you ever did was to shout, rage and storm at anyone who crossed you. Now you're totally uncomprehending and completely surprised that the Cabinet, the Party, the Media and in fact absolutely EVERYONE has turned against you. At last, it's eventually dawned on all of them that whatever it was they once saw in you at the beginning of your premiership has since quickly evaporated. They all realize – too late now – that you should never have stepped into my shoes. Oh yes Gordon, you're PM alright, but you've no real charisma. You're just a schoolyard bully who nobody's afraid of anymore."

"But you promoted me, you kept me in office – my mistakes are also your mistakes."

"Did I really have a choice, Gordon? Could I have afforded to leave you to glower on the backbenches, endlessly plotting against me – waiting for me to slip so you could take over? No Gordon, it was better to keep you in the Cabinet where you could take the blame for any economic downturn. In reality, I knew you never amounted to much when you allowed me to become Party Leader. A real man would have fought far harder for the position."

"But you promised that I would be your successor."

"Did you really mistake my vague assurances for a promise?"

"But you kept on promising and never delivering."

"Were you really that naive to believe in my promises? If so, I pity you. Why do you think I kept delaying my resignation? I did owe something to this country by preventing you from getting to *'number ten'* and ruining everything, as I knew you would."

"But you promised and promised!"

"There you go Gordon. You always viewed power as an entitlement for what, at best, was a very grudging loyalty. You could never see that, in democracy, power has to be earned; you must entice people to trust in you, no matter how groundless that trust is. You have to create the impression that you're a *'regular sort of guy'* who's not simply the best but the <u>only</u> man for the job. Soon, neither the Party nor the people will need to tolerate you any longer. Your use will be at an end. You think no one else wants the job but in the end somebody always wants it. There'll be someone out there biding his time to fill your shoes. You never understood these points but Cameron is beginning to. He's a fast learner, skilfully beginning to follow my example."

"That Tory!!! You want him in power to continue your legacy!"

"Of course! Do you think I owe the Labour Party a debt of gratitude after they got rid of me, despite winning three General Elections for them? You, Gordon, are my best revenge on Labour, and also you're a punishment on the British Public who never did appreciate my policies on Iraq."

"That was your mess and your mess alone, Tony!"

"Was it Gordon? I don't recall you making any principled resignation speeches at the time. All you did was to sit on the sidelines hoping I would come crashing down."

"You... you!!!"

"Now, now Gordon, there's no telephone to throw at me in this dream. That temper of yours has always been a weakness – one which I thought it best to tolerate at the time. I wanted to give you plenty of time to make enemies who would then come to see my own Premiership in a more favourable light. It was an old trick of the Roman Caesars to appoint a man they knew would be worse than themselves so that their reputation would be viewed more favourably in history. Yet all I did was to give the Labour Party what they and you wanted. In your usual clumsy fashion, you're trying the same trick with that fawning courtier Ed Balls. He must be bad if you think he's even worse than you. Even by *my* standards he's reptilian and to know his name is to know the quality of his economic arguments. Ed Milibrand and he make a pretty pair in your government – one is your *'yes'* man the other is your *'hatchet'* man. No wonder you required the services of Peter Mandelson!"

"You *'set me up!'*"

"No Gordon, I only allowed you to *'set yourself up.'* It was your decision to aspire for the top job – one which you were totally unequipped to fill in terms of temperament or ability. You never possessed an ounce of humility ever to accept this. Despite seeing Cameron's performance in the House you never had the common sense to ask yourself, *'Am I really up to this job?'* His jibes I could always smile away, but you would bottle them up and choke with envy at his superior political talents – just as you used to choke at mine. The problem with you is that you could never tolerate anyone being better than you at anything. You hate Cameron for the same reason you hated me; jealousy. Very quickly the public came to see that you amounted to nothing more than an envious usurper, unable to offer them anything – not even a fake smile."

"You were always good at that, Tony."

"Yes, but I could offer them a whole lot more – like the feeling that I knew where I was going. I couldn't walk on water but I always tried to give the impression that I could."

"I did believe that you did think you could..."

"That's the point Gordon, in politics impressions matter but you could never see that."

"But at least I had substance."

"What substance? An economy near bankruptcy, a society near collapse, an underequipped army, RAF planes that blow-up, an overinflated bureaucracy which we can barely maintain? All these in areas for which I gave you the responsibility – indeed, I had no choice but to let you have your own way as you had such strong support from the less astute sections of the Labour Party. You never even told me what you were doing most of time and now everything you've touched has been a failure with a capital *'F,'* in history books you'll be remembered as *'Wrecker'* or *'Ruin'* Brown – the worst Prime Minister this country has ever had. National bankruptcy will be your legacy.

"Grrr!"

"There you go into one of your inarticulate rages – but remember, in dreams you can't hit people. Your jealousy for my superior abilities flared into outright hatred – not least because I was such a convincing winner. I *'played'* the electorate so well and this is something you can't even begin to do. I look forward to seeing your face on the day that Cameron strolls into Number Ten. It'll remind you of me, when I, and not you, entered through that self-same door. My wife, Cherie, will be especially delighted – she never did like you."

"But at least I have principles – unlike you or that money-grabbing wife of yours."

"'Oh, come on! What principles you thought you possessed have long since disappeared – having my old Spin Doctor *'Mandy'* back in the cabinet shows that. I'm really glad he took my advice to accept your offer of a ministerial job; he'll ensure that you'll politically destruct in a more satisfying way whilst he, of course, will personally appear utterly blameless. The way you begged him to return quite proves my point about you needing me all along. I'm unavailable because I'm busy with more important global affairs, so off you go vying for the next best option in having my old *'number two.'* Most touching."

"At least I really cared about having a fair society, I never wasted time fawning over celebrities and hanging around with dubious business cronies."

"*'Cared'* – in the past tense – as I wish your premiership was now! Your care for the poor was shown by the abolition of the 10% tax rate to make short term electoral gain. Your answer to every problem was to *'centralize and spend'* with the result that now nothing is left. *'The cupboard is bare'* to quote the Tory Shadow Chancellor. The result of your policies has been to make this country's economy vulnerable to shock. Thanks to you what could have been a bad dose of flu from America has now become double pneumonia. It could finish this country, never mind your reputation, such as it is. Your answer to every economic problem was to spend and get into debt. I just wonder when the International Monetary Fund will be called in."

"They were our policies"

"Only up to the point I had to tolerate them in order to preserve the unity of the Labour Party. Maybe I should have been firmer but at least I tried to move this country forward in the right direction, despite your attempts to constantly thwart me."

"You... you!"

"Now put down that big clunking fist of yours, you can't hit a figment of your imagination."

"I wish you were just that."

"The truth is, Gordon, you've betrayed everything you once stood for. Envy has eaten away at your own principles."

"You led me into this!"

"But you freely chose to abandon your principles, unlike others of a higher calibre. They resigned from high office, knowing it was best for the Party. But you – you barged ahead, stubbornly determined to take the path that would make you into an *'empty shell'* politician. Why, you're now as vacuous as me! Be careful who you envy, Gordon; because you risk becoming just like them! However, unlike me, you never did rest easy in your lies; you always looked so unhappy when you betrayed people (except when it was me of course) or when you were *'selling this country out'* to Europe. It must be something to do with your strict Scottish Presbyterian background. I freely admit deception never did come naturally to you - when you try it you're about as convincing as a *'speak your weight'* machine.'"

"It came naturally enough to you, Tony."

"Oh yes, but I could always see the fun side of hoodwinking people, especially if there was some gain to be had in it. *'Spin'* can be a bit of a lark really but this is something you've never grasped. With you it was different, that's why I encouraged you to stay outside of the media spotlight. Rule one with the media is *'to realize* that they never deserve to be told the truth,' and rule two is to 'only tell the truth when you absolutely have to and even then keep it vague.' These are two of the three main rules of *'spin.'*"

"And the third?"

"*'Keep unelectable ministers away from the public gaze.'* This was a policy I followed with you Gordon, to keep you from frightening people."

"Doubtless with Mandy's connivance."

"Of course, too much media attention would have made you a liability in my government. You're not doing so well – now that you're bang smack in the middle of the spotlight? Did you think the electorate liked to hear you spouting off all that treasury *'guff?'* Twice a year at the Budget and Annual Chancellor's speech was more than enough."

"The trouble was, Tony, that you never had any sense of responsibility."

"On the contrary Gordon, I only abdicated my responsibility when I allowed you to become Prime Minister in my place. With regard to Iraq I was very responsible."

"Try telling that to the Iraqis you've bombed."

"But at least I could make decisions. I'll leave behind a positive legacy."

"What legacy! You've left nothing but…"

"David Cameron! He's the man to finish the job I set out to do in reforming the public sector. After you, he's my best vengeance on that ungrateful Labour Party. I know that every time you confront him you're going to hear my voice, see my face and feel that all-consuming envy. You're defeated Gordon – but I didn't defeat you – all I did was to have allowed you to defeat yourself. Only the current financial crisis is keeping you in power. Remember, it was you who initiated that coup against me and wore that idiotic smirk when you knew you'd be Prime Minister in my place. However, you forgot that in politics you should be very careful what you aim for because you might just get it and in your case Gordon you certainly have!"

"But, Tony!"

"Don't *'but Tony'* me; it's a bit late for that now. The fact is Gordon, you've always hated me because you've always needed me; without me you're nothing – a complete nonentity. I'm going to enjoy watching your face as the results of the next election come in, relishing your downfall and your consignment to the *'living death'* of public disgrace. Without me, you'll revert to being the failure you've always been. Don't expect any prestigious positions at the IMF or World Bank. If he's any sense Cameron will veto such moves when he gets to number ten. Despite your attempts to save the world banking system, you'll be remembered as the worst Labour Prime Minister since Ramsey MacDonald."

"Please! Can you help me, Tony?"

"What! Help you out of the hole you've dug for yourself! You'll be asking me to be your Deputy Prime Minister next! The trouble is you've always lacked democratic legitimacy; it was you yourself, not the people, who put you into Number Ten. You chose to steal my job, which I'd been elected to do."

"But everything's falling apart now!"

"That's not my responsibility."

"Tony, Tony, Tony, don't vanish on me – at least leave those gold bars behind, I'll need them to shore-up the economy – Tony, Tony, please don't go TONY – Aaargh!"

"What is it dear? You almost kicked me out of bed."

"I've just had a bad dream about Tony"

"Not another one!"

"He's become the conscience that haunts me."

"Get to sleep my dear – you've got that important meeting"

"I know, I know, but what would Tony do?"

"Hush! Hush! He's gone, you're in charge now."

"Am I? Am I really?"[145]

---

[145] This dialogue was written on the morning of Monday, 29th September 2008 and updated on Wednesday, 1st June 2011.

THE MUCHWORTH ROOM

One cold and wet autumnal evening
As grey pallid light
Faded into an inky black night
I waivered near the entrance
Of an old Community Hall
Searching for a particular meeting
That wasn't there
A heavy cumbersome capstone
Arched above the doorway
With the word *'BOYS'*
Chiselled deeply into its surface
By a long-since forgotten workman
The realization dawned that this building
Had once been my old Primary School
Well here it was
Proudly grand, Victorian and Gothic in its design

I stepped back into the old playground –
The scene of many a fight
And saw once more
The grim, smog besmirched walls
And there on high
The empty bell tower
Now standing as muted witness
To a bygone age
When subdued children
Would stream into two separate entrances
One for the *'BOYS'*
The other for the *'GIRLS'*
Leaving behind
A bevy of half relieved and half anxious mothers
At the schoolyard gate

In the hallway
The smell of briskly rubbed-in floor polish
Stirred a whole jumble of memories,
Which stilled suddenly upon hearing
A voice inside the old Assembly Hall,

A Marshall Arts' instructor
Barking his orders in broken Chinese lingo
Accompanied by grunts, wheezes
And thudding sounds upon the floor

And then another sound –
This time calm and melodious
The gentle piping of a flute
Whose notes resonated pleasantly in the air
'Must be some type of relaxation class,' I thought

Yet my attention was caught
By a loud rhythmic chanting
Somewhere further down the corridor
Mindless, mystical mantras
Tumbling out into the autumnal evening air
Promising a *'magical mystery tour'*
To a nowhere Nirvana
*'I presume that's the meditation group –
What a din!'*
They're meeting in my old class room.'

I stood pensive and still, quietly contemplating all around me

In contrast to the musty Victorian browns
And faded creams of my childhood
Everything was now
A *'politically correct'* green
The doors a verdant grass hue
And the walls a pallid mint,
Only the smell of the floor polish
Connected me tangibly with my distant childhood landscape

I chanced to glance to my left
And there, affixed to a door
Just below waist height,
Shone a polished brass nameplate
And engraved upon it, in slim black script writing
Were the words, *'The Muchworth Room'*

'Ah! The old headmaster's study!
I inwardly shuddered
Many a poor kid had got a right old thrashing in there,
'Masher Muchworth' had certainly known
How to use his cane!'

Suddenly, I could feel myself
Sinking, down, down, down
Down through a deep turquoise
Pool of memory,
Sinking back and back and back for 42 years
To resurface,
As a nine year old boy –
Gasping for air
As I ran around a tarmac playground
In schoolboy shorts
And NHS spectacles
Pretending to be James Bond
Or some other *'action hero'*

I was back in the early summer of 1965
When pop music was very much alive
And even the Rolling Stones looked young
Coronation Street was the favourite *'Soap'*
Featuring a traditional working class life
That would fade with the old industries
Of coal, steel and cloth

Young men, the despair
Of their war-veteran fathers
Still sporting *'Teddy boy'* quiffs
And trying to develop a fragile manhood
By exercising with chest expanders
Stopping only to squeeze out the puss
From their acne spots

Young women, the despair
Of their Blitz-surviving mothers
Sporting the beehive hair style
And pouting loud red lipstick

Wearing increasingly short skirts
In order to show that
They dedicated followers of fashion

Working class men
With bitter war memories
Wearing cloth caps
(Middle class men, trilbies)
Their wives skilfully keeping rollers in place
Using *'Ena Sharples'* hairnets and clips
In order to add to their *'battle-axe'* look

In those days, smoking was a fact of life
And only the Beetles film *'Help'*
Hinted of the narcotic-drenched future yet to come
Where Eastern Gurus would enjoy a media credibility
Formerly reserved for TV vicars and bishops;
Dr Who was then a white-haired grumpy old man
Fighting Daleks and Monsters
Rather than a trendy quick-witted young man
Delivering postmodern irony
(And still fighting Daleks and Monsters)

As for Vietnam
It was a far away country
About which we cared little
And computers were something
That took up the room space
Of large military organizations
Or the cavernous, neon-lit basements
Of well-endowed universities
Seen only by the public in science-fiction films
Or futuristic TV shows

Summer of '65,
Where 'Fish *'n'* Chips was the only *'take away'*
The last age of innocence –
Before the nation was shocked
By those children's bodies found
On Saddleworth Moor

And the British Public still believed in
Prime Minister Harold Wilson's promise
Of a better society
Many thought that government planning
Would solve every problem
And that *'High-Rise'* Council Estates
Would be the harbingers of a New Jerusalem
Rather than the Hells they were to become

'Sing up, boy
Sing up!'

'I'm trying sir,
But the others are drowning out my voice'
'Now sing-up
Otherwise I'll drown you!'
In frightened obedience I complied
Provoking the other boys and girls in my class
To raucous laughter
'Not very bright now, are we?'
Sing-up
Sing LOUDLY'
Otherwise, see me in my study!'

Once I complied
More laughter
'SILENCE!'
One boy continued smirking
For just a little too long
'See me in my study tomorrow morning, during break'
The smirk vanished into a tearful, circus clown expression
'Any more want to visit my study?'

Silence

'Good, carry on with the music lesson Miss Holmes
I don't want to hear any more laughter from this room
Teach young Smith here to sing properly
He sounds like a bullfrog with laryngitis'
Muchworth turned abruptly and strode out

Leaving a flustered Miss Holmes
To carry on as best she could

Muchworth was small in stature
Plump and balding
With parchment-coloured skin
Which would suddenly flush crimson
When provoked to anger
An ugly wart protruded from his right cheek
And his lips were often pursed, straight and set
He wore a faded chequered sports jacket
Complete with sewn-on elbow patches
Looking for all the world like it had come from a jumble sale

Word had it that he'd been after
The *'Headship'* of a larger, more prestigious school
But nothing had come of this
And all his hopes were dashed
All that had remained was
A frustrated sense of bitter disappointment and
And an angry, seething inner resentment
Which continued to smoulder on and on
Erupting in short, barely controlled outbursts
When least expected

Next day I saw the boy who had smirked
Standing hushed and pale outside the study-door
Too fearful even to cry
From inside the room came the swishing
Of a rapidly descending cane
And the resounding *'thwack'*
On another unfortunate boy's *'backside'*

'That could have been me!' I thought
As I hurriedly entered the safety of a large classroom
Shoving half a bagful of plain crisps
(The ones containing little blue bags of salt)
Into the pocket of my shorts

A few days later Miss Primwell, the school secretary
Bustled into my classroom
In the middle of me trying to *'do some sums'*
She was a gangly, *'fifty something'* woman
Unmarried and always on a diet
She wore severe, black horn-rimmed glasses
Astride a prominent beaky nose
On this particular day she was wearing
A very neat black skirt and matching top
In place of her usual garb of spinsterish tweeds

'Miss Holmes, Mr Muchworth
Would like to see Richard Smith in his study,
She briskly announced
A wave of pity flowed across the whole of my class
'What had I done? What had I done?'

Unlike many others I'd escaped the cane
Always too busy with my nose in a Ladybird History book
Or a Children's Encyclopaedia
To be the cause of any trouble
A look of quiet concern from Miss Holmes, then
'You'd better go, you can finish your sums later'
A note of resigned compassion in her voice

'What had I done? What had I done?'

The tight lump in my throat
Fell to cause a knot in my stomach
I wanted so much to wee!

I tried desperately to *'mentally escape'*
Back to a happy summer's day in Calais
Where I'd visited with my parents
On a day-trip; away from a bug-infested
Guest House in Herne Bay, Kent
Where myself and other children had giggled
At the creepy male proprietor who'd we'd nicknamed *'The Spectre'*

I was aware
Even during that holiday
That there was this bald yet funny Russian man
Called Khrushchev who was headmaster
Of a very strict school called the Soviet Union
He could scare people even more than Mr Muchworth;
Something about *'Cuba'* my parents had said
Miss Primwell tapped politely on the study door
'Come in' called a voice, full of contrived *'bonhomie'*
I blinked and wondered
'Could that really be Mr Muchworth?'

Miss Primwell opened the door,
There, wearing a neat black suit
Sat Mr Muchworth, glowing – but not glowering!
His *'set'* smile revealing
A row of yellow nicotine-stained teeth;
Flanked on either side of him stood two men
Each wearing a stern school inspector's look
As I stood bemused and dumbfounded
At the scene before me
Mr Muchworth positively beamed in my direction
'This boy is an example of the progress we've made
He's one of our brightest pupils
And we've just been informed that he's passed
The Grammar School Entrance Exam
And begins there next term
He's a testimony to the skill of our staff
– I personally gave him extra lessons –
His performance is a credit to the whole school."
Once more his face broke into a cheery smile
(Something I'd never seen before)
'Now didn't we all do well, Smithy?'
He said in a self-important but ingratiating tone
'Yes Sir' I replied
Baffled by this *'out of character'* adult display
I had been childishly pondering throughout our brief exchange;
'Why did he call me Smiffy,
He's that dumb kid in the Bash Street Kids?'
The inspectors continued to watch intently,

Showing no glimmer of emotion in their flint-like faces
Please show him out Miss Primwell
And make sure he receives that book as a reward'
Was I seeing things?
'Did Miss Primwell actually smile at Mr Muchworth
As she briskly ushered me from the room?
What secret had they between them? Was she poorly?
Mr Muchworth never makes anyone happy!'

The next day I was paraded like a triumphant trophy
Before the whole School Assembly
Muchworth (still in his black suit) standing and proclaiming
In near-jovial tones
'Now *if, like Smithy here, you work hard*
Some of you could pass the 'eleven plus'
And enjoy the privilege of a Grammar School Education,
To become famous Doctors, Scientists and Statesmen
And be a great credit to society
You could put the 'Great' back into 'Great Britain!'
Smithy here offers us all hope, that from little acorns big trees can grow...'
, somewhat bemused I wondered why other staff members
Looked like Miss Primwell had done yesterday
With *'set smiles'* stuck on their faces,
'Were they getting poorly too?'
In my hand I clutched my reward
A book on algebra by Dr Myles Muchworth
The elder brother of our Mr Muchworth
Someone *'big'* in education at Oxford and London

Suddenly, the 1960's Primary School vista
Dissolved before my eyes
Like a lump of sugar in water,
I sank through the Assembly Hall floor
To emerge once more outside the old study door
Now a Manager's office
Complete with laptop computer
And wireless access to the Internet

*'Yes! I'd made it
Here I was at fifty one
In late October 2007;
I had indeed attended the Grammar School
And gone on into Further Education
Becoming much more qualified in that field
Than Mr Muchworth had ever been'*

It was perhaps best that
He'd never been informed
That I'd only been accepted by the Grammar School
Because my family had attended there for three generations
In normal circumstances,
(So my parents had been told
By the Junior School Headmaster of the day)
They would never have let in anyone with my disappointing showing
Especially as Muchworth's school
Hadn't even taught me to write properly,
However, my parents had been regular fee payers
For my older brother
And my father and his father before him
Had been pupils there
So I'd been given the benefit of the doubt.

Only in my twenty eighth year did
I begin to acquire intelligence
Everything before that had just been knowledge

Before leaving
I looked again at the nameplate
Remembering that Muchworth
Had suddenly died of a stroke in 1976
Shortly after his retirement;
It had taken everyone by surprise because he'd looked so well
And was looking forward to a holiday in Italy

Now just a long forgotten name
On a shiny brass plate

'What a life!
What pretence!
What a bully of a man!'

Suddenly, from behind the door
I could distinctly hear the swishing of a cane[146]

---

[146] This story was written on Wednesday, 12th December 2007. It expresses how the past and present can interact through memory. It went though several re-drafts before being completed on Tuesday, 2nd September 2008.

WHITBY STORM

Having spent a few pleasant hours in Robin Hood's Bay, my husband Richard and I we decided to head back to Whitby along the designated coastal footpath known as the *'The Cleveland Way.'* It was about 5 o'clock and we reckoned we'd get back to our Youth Hostel for about seven in the evening.

We set off at a fairly brisk pace, just making out the rumbling of thunder far ahead of us and seeing a dark bank of clouds moving steadily in our direction. We'd no sooner begun when we met two young women walking our way, looking obviously pleased with themselves at getting further away from the storm. They were laughing together in a *'chummy'* sort of way- after all they were nearly *'home'* – we were just beginning.

We walked briskly on with the storm coming ever closer. Suddenly our hearts jumped as sheet lightening lit up the whole sky and jagged bolts crazily zigzagged their way to earth. I pulled my sunhat slightly over my eyes (rather like an ostrich trying to bury its own head). I was determined not to see the lightning streaks, which I found to be both awe-inspiring and hugely terrifying all at the same time.

Meanwhile, the storm continued to move determinedly our way. We were hoping it would move off to our right and out into the sea, but *'oh no,'* it seemed menacingly to hover and brood just off to our left, totally unwilling to budge. Each successive lightening crack made us nearly jump out of our skins and we rapidly *'upped'* our walking pace – becoming ever more desperate to see the Caravan Park which we knew nestled by the cliff edge – itself a sure sign that Whitby (and our Youth Hostel) were just another thirty minutes away.

We wondered whether to linger in the *'wykes'* we came across until the storm abated, but because we were making good progress we decided to carry on. At last the longed-for Caravan Park came into view, the sight of which galvanised us into action. We shot up a *'lightening quick'* prayer and began running madly! I outran Richard all too easily (he would later claim that his backpack had been heavier than mine). However, I could still hear him behind me loudly voicing some doom-laden comment as another flash lit up the sky with a further crash of thunder. Come to think of it – even at the beginning of the storm Richard had been all too quick to give me unasked-for information about the storm's ferocity. He seemed to have taken some sort of morbid delight in telling me how terribly EXPOSED WE WERE on top of the cliff-edge. My only rejoinder then – and now, was to yell back at him, *'Richard, shut up!'* (My line of reasoning being that if you can't say anything helpful, then don't say it at all.)

And so we madly raced along for two separate quarter mile stretches – stopping only to catch our breath before rushing off. At one stage the lightning seemed so near (zigzagging behind Whitby Abbey) that I pulled my sun hat even further down, desperate not to see the *'lightning bolt'* that was sure to kill me outright. (I even contemplated visions of Richard trying to resuscitate me – kiss of life and all that). Hmmm, I may as well own up to it now that I shamefacedly held onto a 10p coin that was in my pocket at the time. Should I throw it away as I ran along the cliff path? No way! I mean 10p was 10p after all! (And who said Yorkshire folk were the meanest!) I was determined to hang on to it even though I knew deep down that it had the potential to be a mini-lightning conductor. That 10p could quite literally have been the death of me. But part with it – throw it away – good gracious – no!

We continued our mad run – with me still way ahead of Richard. I quickly looked back in his direction as I ran past the boundary fence of the Caravan Park; he seemed so very far away. I darted through an open doorway and straight into a video games room. Two children were busily engaged in front of a flashing computer screen. They turned and looked at me, blandly asking, *"Is there thunder outside?"* *"Yes!"* I replied, in a croaking, heaving, rasping voice. It was about the only word I could utter at the time because my breathing was so laboured – in fact I sounded like a braying donkey (or as Richard would later remark – *"puffing like a steam engine"*). I remember, even then, thinking it strange that these boys looked so very disinterested and *'disconnected.'* Here I was in such an awful physical state (no exaggeration – I really was) and they seemed not to be registering this at all. Instead, their attention had quickly been recaptured by the computer screen and I was left standing, sweaty faced with my chest heaving as I laboured to regain my breath. I popped my head out of the open doorway looking for Richard to arrive. What seemed a long time passed when at last I saw him and he ran toward me, all red-faced and wheezing dreadfully. He'd no sooner entered the games room when both spotted an empty and brightly lit room opposite and we made a mad dash for it, not wishing to upset any more children who might enter the games room. After all, we must have looked and sounded a little odd – with our faces a bright beetroot red, our breathing loud and laboured and both of us steaming with sweat. In fact we must have looked very nearly inhuman – like visitors from another planet.

This other room turned out to be the Caravan Park's launderette. We lingered by its doorway, watching the rain as it only now began to pour down. Just to our right was a huge mirror which accurately reflected the totally spent physical state we were in. I'd certainly never before (nor since) seen us both looking this dreadful. I was shocked to see how puce and sweaty our faces really were and how harsh and laboured our breathing sounded. Thankfully, within about ten minutes our breathing had steadied and our faces had resumed their normal colour. I heaved myself up onto a broad shelf – letting my legs dangle freely, but Richard (in a rather gloomy and foreboding manner) decided that we'd best move to the back of the room, as far from the open doorway as possible; (this was because lightning bolts were still in evidence outside).

Earlier that afternoon whilst we'd both wandered around Robin Hood's bay, we'd stopped at a second-hand bookshop and had bought some good books from the lovely lady bookseller there. She'd unfortunately been on the *'receiving end'* of one of Richard's attempts to advertise his own websites and I remember having admired her patience and smiling forbearance. Now we each took a book from our rucksacks and settled down to read – getting up only occasionally to stretch our legs and to see how the storm was doing. Time ticked by as we gradually became absorbed – each in our own literary world. However, the rumbles and flashes outside continued unabated, even momentarily cutting off power to the lights. I was reading Mike Harding's book entitled, *'Rambling On'* which was a light-hearted look at the sort of people who make-up a typical rambling club. I had reached page 41 where he was humorously criticising *'The Romantic Rambler'* who, he said, *forever writes verses of a pastoral nature."* He then remarked *"It goes on like this for hundreds of lines and is as interesting as a night out at the launderette."* Well, I read this last line out loud to Richard and we both laughed uproariously because here we were – virtual prisoners inside a launderette where we desperately hoped we wouldn't have to spend the night! The whole scenario seemed just a little crazy! We gradually calmed down and settled ourselves down again to our former pattern of reading, getting up, looking outside, sitting down, reading and getting up again. Eventually we could finally see the sky beginning to clear and to take on a lighter hue. The storm clouds, at long last, appeared to be drifting out to sea. We packed our books away, donned our rucksacks and left the launderette, relieved to be heading back to our hostel – albeit in a light smattering of rain. It was an uneventful return – as if nothing at all untoward had happened throughout the previous few hours. I think we entered the Youth Hostel just after eight o'clock – only about an hour or so after our due destination time.

The following day was sunny enough for us to enjoy a swim in the sea at Whitby before travelling on to Beverley. As we lingered on the beach we could hear people speaking into their mobile phones, describing the ordeals they'd endured the previous day. We could hear how tents had been flooded and children campers driven to hysterical screaming. How a local television mast had been struck by lightning and much of the village of Helmsley flooded out too. After hearing of the absolute terror that others had endured we decided that our little saunter on the cliff top hadn't really been nearly so bad after all!

Since writing this piece, I've wished to somehow capture something of the essence of the forces unleashed that afternoon. My overall impression was that Nature, unleashed in all of her fury, had simply *'found us out.'* There we were upon the cliff top – frail dots of humanity, completely expressed to Nature's overpowering fury and passion – and all we could do was to fervently hope and pray. In our simplicity we had expected God either to take care of us or allow us to die – it felt at the time as if there was no middle ground.

We were fortunate in that circumstances had been in our favour – with us finding a safe haven in the Caravan Park. Nevertheless, we'd had to wait upon Nature's good pleasure until the storm had abated and we'd dared to re-assert ourselves as human beings. Her dreadful might and majesty had completely dwarfed our perception of ourselves – of our place upon the planet. Our final dependence had lain with God Himself, the maker of Heaven and Earth – of thunder and lightning, stillness and calm. The absolute beauty and awe-inspiring magnificence of His Creation had been made very real to us. Surely, *"The heavens declare the glory of God; and the firmament shows his handiwork,"* (Psalm 19:1). Ah yes, I'm now sounding all *'holier than thou'* - I assure you nothing could be further from the truth. A Christian I most certainly am, a devout one I am not ... I could go on and on ... but I won't![147]

---

[147] The following account was written by June, my wife, and describes an incident which took place on Sunday, 19th June 2005 and which subsequently provided the setting for my poem *'Flash, Crash, Dash!'* The word *'wyke'* is a Yorkshire term for a steep, tree-lined gulley, with a small stream often running through it.

PART G: TEACHING AIDS

(Resources which may benefit students of poetry)

HOW TO INTERPRET POETRY

An effective way to interpret a poem is to read through it carefully (at least two or three times) before asking the following questions: -

1) What first impressions did the poem create?
2) Was the poem easy or difficult to understand?
3) When was the poem written?
4) What was the poem's context (or setting)?
5) Where was it written?
6) Who wrote it and were they famous?
7) What political or other constraints existed when it was written?
8) Why was it written?
9) What was the poet's personal background?
10) Was the poet pursuing a secret agenda?
11) Who was the original intended audience?
12) Was the audience homogeneous or mixed?
13) Was the poem distinctly comical, didactic, metaphysical, pastoral, satirical or tragic?
14) Was the poem action, character or idea-centred?
15) Did the poem tell a story (narrative)?
16) Was the narrative linear or circular?
17) Did the poem convey a message?
18) What was the poem's basic philosophy (or belief system)?
19) How coherent was its philosophy?
20) Who could benefit or be harmed by this philosophy?
21) Was the poem markedly biased in favour of or against something?
22) How strong was its bias?
23) Did it adopt a first or third person viewpoint?
24) What tone was adopted?
25) Did the tone change and if so why?
26) Was it in *'fixed'* or *'free'* verse form?
27) How many verses were there?
28) Were the verses regular or irregular?
29) Were the verses rhyming or non-rhyming?
30) Was there a rhythmic beat to the poem?
31) Was the style ornate, formal, informal or colloquial?
32) What was the prevailing mood (or emotion) in the poem?
33) Did the prevailing mood change and why?

34) Were visual representations (*e.g.* photographs) used in the poem?
35) Were stylistic devices employed *e.g.* alliterations or assonances?
36) Were metaphors and similes used to create imagery?
37) Were specific linguistic devices used *e.g.* onomatopoeia?
38) Was a *'persona'* adopted?
39) Was *'animation'* used?
40) What embedded facts, (if any) lay hidden within the poem?
41) Was the poem pure fantasy?
42) What did the poem mean?
43) Have both explicit and implicit meanings been considered?
44) Were there any alternative interpretations?
45) Why were alternative interpretations accepted (or rejected)?
46) What would the original audience have felt about the poem?
47) How did the poem make me feel and why?
48) Could the poem be summarised in a couple of sentences?
49) Did the poem achieve what it set out to do?
50) Could the poet have done better and if so, how?
51) What lessons could be learnt from the poem?
52) Would I like to read the poem again?
53) What score out of ten would I give the poem, and why?

Where possible try to enter the mind of the poet and feel what he or she felt – even though it may be fairly depressing. Also, the use of relevant quotations and supporting evidence add clarity to any given answer. The examiner would expect the reader to fully engage with and respond to a poem on a personal as well as an intellectual level. However, not all of the following questions need be asked about every poem. The meaning of key terms will be found in a standard dictionary or textbook on poetry.

HOW TO ASSESS A POEM

The following questions should enable a poet to increase his/her capacity to receive constructive criticism in relation to their own poetry. The first block of questions asks whether the poem has displayed particular strengths, whilst the second discovers whether it has avoided particular weaknesses. Represented is a somewhat formal approach which may not suit everyone, but it should be useful for beginners and those wishing to systematically assess poetry. Practical analytical and critical skills are essential to writing good poetry.[148]

1) Has this poem adequately demonstrated: -
1.1 Why was it written?
1.2 For whom has it been written?
1.3 Where and when was it set?
1.4 Whether it adopted a didactic or hedonistic approach?
1.5 Whether it followed a universal or particular theme?
1.6 The ability to stir appropriate emotions?
1.7 A clear (either circular, linear or narrative) structure?
1.8 A consistent viewpoint?
1.9 A sufficient vocabulary?
1.10 An appropriate use of formal or informal language?
1.11 A capacity to convey an intended mood?
1.12 A suitable style that fits the subject matter?
1.13 A skilful use of imagery?
1.14 A talent for using helpful literature devices e.g. personification and rhetorical questions?
1.15 An ability to display interesting ideas?
1.16 A wise sensitivity to its subject matter?
1.17 Either topical or historical awareness?
1.18 Courage in tackling controversial issues?
1.19 A tendency to provoke discussion and thought?
1.20 An appropriate use of humour?
1.21 A vivid characterisation of people, place and setting?
1.22 Evidence of learning from previous poetical traditions?
1.23 An attractive, eye-catching format?
1.24 Some originality?
1.25 An appropriate length?

---

[148] Most of the questions were devised in May 2005 after the author had reviewed the extensive criticism he'd personally received during his time on a certain Internet poetry discussion forum.

1.26 Evidence of careful revision?
1.27 A strong, rather than a vague, or meandering close?
1.28 An ability to provoke either a *'wow'* or *'I've learned something useful'* reaction?
1.29 An entertainment and/or educational function?
1.30 A capacity to leave the reader wanting more?

2) Has this poem avoided the following mistakes: -
2.1 A failure to display previously listed strengths?
2.2 Lack of clarity?
2.3 Irritating self-pity?
2.4 The employment of too many clichés?
2.5 Inappropriate language?
2.6 Unoriginal imagery and phraseology?
2.7 Redundant phrases and adjectives?
2.8 Superficial comments?
2.9 Gross insensitivity?
2.10 Trite superficiality?
2.11 Unnecessary repetition?
2.12 Adding too many explanations and comments
2.13 Inappropriate line breaks?
2.14 Boring, annoying or baffling phraseology?
2.15 Rambling on for too long?
2.16 A failure to leave enough to the imagination?
2.17 Serious factual mistakes?
2.18 Pretentious pomposity?
2.19 A hectoring style, which arrogantly tells the reader what they should or should not think?
2.20 The use of outdated satire?
2.21 The incitement of religious, racial or political hatred?
2.22 A weak ending?

ADVICE TO A YOUNG POET

To any young aspiring poet my advice is this;
Begin developing your talents in solitude
Let the pen write in an act of spontaneous creation
Don't worry if what you produce is of indifferent quality
The time for self-assessment has not yet come
Be patient, we all have to begin somewhere –
Even with inane scribbling
Which later we may find utterly embarrassing

Remember, it's best to begin writing about something you know
Before branching off into other areas
Once you <u>have</u> begun writing
Check your work carefully
Learn to draft and re-draft it
Also know when to lay it aside
And return to it later with a fresh mind

In order to further develop your talent
Try out your poems in the company of others
Begin experimenting with new forms
Take account of any feedback
If the same criticism comes from a number of sources
Consider it carefully
And don't be tempted to retreat in a sulk or display a petulant rage
But neither allow such criticism to totally destroy your confidence;
To learn and move on is always a good thing

Should the odd poem be a definite failure
Or you don't obtain the response you wanted from an audience
Avoid fretting – learn from your mistake
And use it as a means to improve your work
Accept that it is through criticism you grow and develop as a poet

As your talent steadily matures
Continue to experiment with new forms
Explore fresh topics
Widen your repertoire
Draw from a variety of cultural sources

And be willing to delve into issues
You wouldn't have dreamt of at an earlier stage

Be thankful if recognition comes your way
But don't allow it to go to your head
Neither expect your poems to win favour with everyone
Above all, don't rely upon poetry as an easy way
Of gaining fame and fortune
To believe that is to become sadly disillusioned

Be wary about becoming obsessed with literary prizes or competitions
For they are often baubles for the vain and insecure
Remember, being a poet is above all a personal vocation
Not a free ticket to wealth and stardom
Or a quick way to gain media attention
Take care to relate to your audience
Yet, be yourself
Act naturally
And avoid vain pretensions
Although a little eccentricity can be a plus

Be willing to try out your poems
With a whole variety of people
Should you, despite your best efforts,
Persistently fail to *'connect'* with an audience
Consider moving on
Never continue performing in front of an audience you dislike
Otherwise you'll be consumed by bitterness
And risk making a public fool of yourself

Never throw endless insults at an audience
For this reveals only a lack of talent and basic good manners
As does singling out defenceless minorities like the disabled
The quickest way to immolate yourself as a performer
Is to joke about rape to a largely female audience
(Especially by suggesting that the victim deserved it)
Or to make light of a serial killer or a child murderer
To do these things can cause unnecessary devastation
And makes you look stupid

In your live performances employ a little showmanship
To add some zest
And to win people's attention
But don't allow the showmanship to take over
Or obscure the content of your poetry
Beware of turning a poetry gig
Into a freak show

In your readings avoid gabling or speaking in a flat monotone
Pause at the right moment to take breath and if necessary
Rehearse in front of a mirror
Don't jump from one poem straight into another

Bring variety into your poetry
Be on the lookout for new techniques and subject matter
Use modern communication technology
To help correct and store your work
But don't be dominated by it
To be endlessly preoccupied with technology can be a huge distraction
As well as a means of frittering away valuable time
First drafts are often better written by hand
Having a good pen available is always helpful

Wherever possible retain the enthusiasm of youth
But gently distil it with the experience of age
Learn from the poets of the past
But take care to understand the day and age in which you <u>now</u> live

Remember, it's unwise to live in a perpetual dreamscape
Or to mistake fantasy for reality
Doing that has been the ruin of many an artist
To go solely by subjective perception is a dangerous thing

As far you are able
Keep mentally and physically fit
Refrain from those bad habits
That can destroy your talents
A creative temperament

Is not an excuse for a lack of discipline
Or irresponsible behaviour
Always go on learning
For the best poets
Are perpetual students of life

As you ripen as a poet
Be thankful for what talent you have
But never be jealous of the talents or honour given to others
If you have the misfortune
Of encountering a brilliant poetical genius
Who effortlessly combines the talents of: -
Shakespeare, Wordsworth and T. S. Elliot
Don't be overwhelmed or lose confidence
Instead, learn from such people
Adopt them as a role model
But avoid slavish imitation
Or any trace of plagiarism[149]
Lest you hear from their lawyer

Avoid the searing vice of envy
For there's no sadder sight
Than an embittered old poet
Being insanely jealous of younger talent
Overtaking them
And gaining more applause
Instead, nurture any new talents
As they begin to emerge
Encourage others
As you'd like to be encouraged
Criticise others
As you would like to be criticised

Be _very_ careful about rushing into publication
For most mainstream publishers can be an endless source of trouble
They will view you as nothing more than a commodity
To be used and then discarded
Whilst others will most assuredly take your money
For doing next to nothing

---

[149] *I.e.* using someone else's work and claiming it as one's own

Self-publication may well be a feasible option
But often involves a mountain of work
Requiring many technical skills
Including a thorough grasp of business practice

Should you become involved with a publisher
Check out their genuine sympathy to the poetical craft
Small publishing houses may be best
But they always seem short of money
Above all, check the background of any publisher <u>extremely</u> carefully
<u>Always read the small print</u>
Of any publishing contract with <u>painstaking</u> care[150]
If in doubt get an outside expert to look at it
Keep in mind the saying *'buyer beware!'*
Check that a publisher's philosophy chimes in with your own
For rarely can parties with opposed value systems
Work harmoniously together

Above all, <u>never</u> resort to a *'Vanity Press'*
For that is a fool's way to get published
Don't pay out large sums of money
For what may well be imaginary services
Never allow the emotional need for publication
To cost you a fortune
Doing that is the way to heartbreak and despair

Be careful if mainstream media attention comes your way
For the media specialises in the destruction,
Rather than the building up, of reputations
Sup with them as you would with the devil
Using a very long spoon
Never expect them to accurately report any story about you

As far as it's up to you
Refrain from pointless literary feuds
For the only winners in such disputes are the lawyers

---

[150] Writer's need to clearly define what is meant by *'out of print.'* There have been instances where publishers regard any work on their data base as being *'in print.'* That way the publisher can cling onto the rights of the book and avoid paying any royalties by publishing it after the author's death. Meanwhile, the poor author is left with nothing except the costly option of seeking legal redress.

In particular, beware of writing scathing reviews
Or of making personal accusations
Unless you can back them up
With evidence that can stand up in a court of law
Assume that every private e-mail you write is in the public domain
For there's no such thing as confidentiality on the internet

Never waste time with futile regrets, saying
'I could have made it to be this or that'
For the only real failure in poetry
Is the failure to use the abilities you have
Popularity may come and go
But a carefully nurtured talent can last for decades

In the end the best advice
I can give to any aspiring poet is this: -
TAKE UP YOUR PEN AND WRITE![151]

---

[151] This series of reflections was first written on Wednesday, 10th August 2011 whilst enduring a choppy ferry crossing from the Isle of Man to Belfast in Northern Ireland.

FURTHER READING

1. Book List

Bennett Andrew and Thomas Peter (2001)
GCSE Total Revision GCSE,
Collins

Burton S. H (1974)
The Criticism of Poetry
Longman

Gardiner Alan (2000)
A-Level Study Guide: English Language
Pearson Education

Fowler G. F & W.H (1993)
The King's English
Wordsworth Books

Harding Mike (1986)
'Rambling On'
Robson Books Ltd, Guild Publishing

Humphry John (2004)
Lost for Words:
The Mangling and Manipulation of the English Language
Hodder & Stoughton

Judson Jerome (1980)
The Poet's Writer's Handbook
Digest Books

Losey D. Frederick, Editor (1937)
The Kingsway Shakespeare
George Harrap & Co Ltd

McDonald Trevor (1999)
Trevor McDonald's World of Poetry
Andre Deutsch, Classics

Marshall Sarah, Editor (2003)
Spotlight Poets
Remus House

Miller Robert & Currie Ian (1976)
The Language of Poetry
Heinemann Educational Books Ltd

Norman Ron & Watkins Anne (2001)
A2 English Language for AQA B
Heinemann

Ross Alison (2001)
AS English Language and Literature for AQA B
Heinemann

Schmidt Michael (2009)
The Great Modern Poets:
An Anthology of the Best Poets Since 1900
Quercus

Truss Lynne (2003)
Eats, Shoots & Leaves:
The Zero Tolerance Approach to Punctuation
Profile Books

Various Authors (2003)
NEAB Anthology
AQA NEAB

Williams Rowan (2002)
The Poems of Rowan Williams
The Perpetua Press, Oxford

2. Booklets

Burke Helen (2007)
Zulu's Petals
Poetry Monthly Press

Marshall Linda (2010)
Half-Moon Glasses
Flux Gallery Press

Stevens Jean (2008)
Undressing in Winter
Matador

READER'S NOTES

www.ingramcontent.com/pod-product-compliance
Lightning Source LLC
Chambersburg PA
CBHW031622160426
43196CB00006B/245